AUTOBIOGRAPHIX

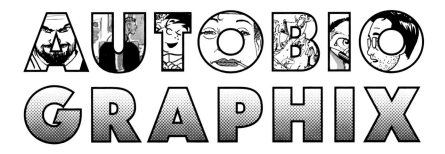

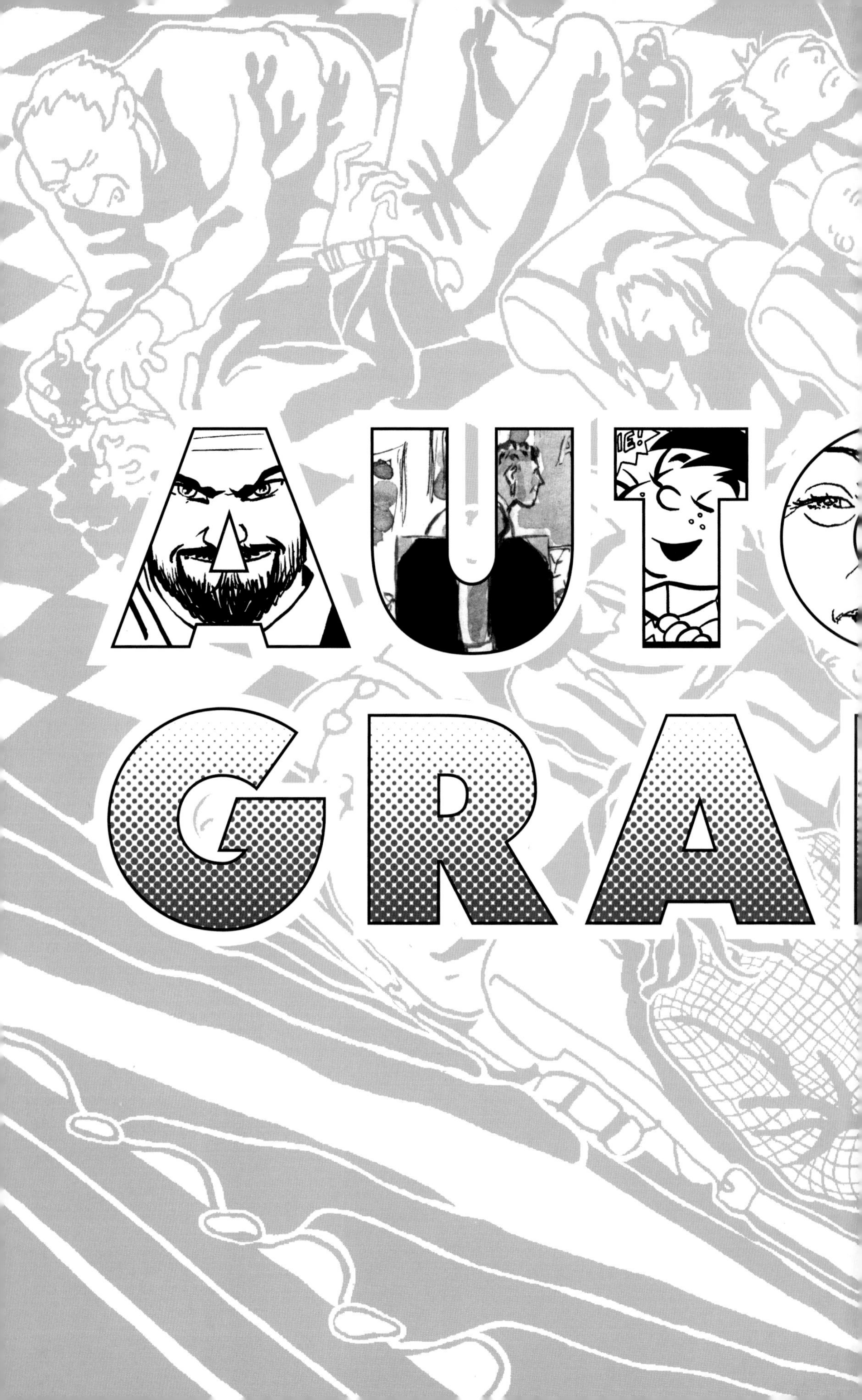
AUT
GRA
IE!

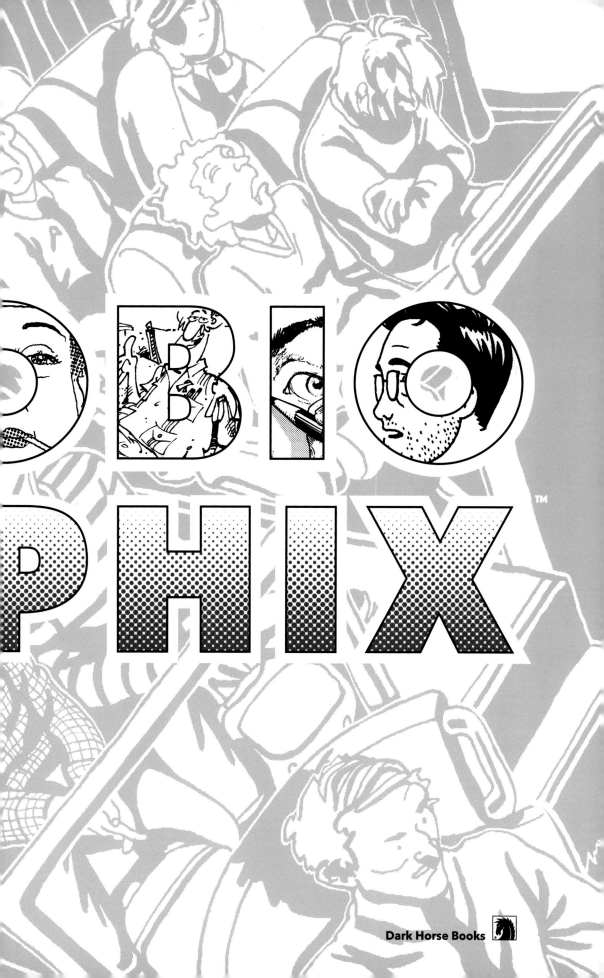

BIO PHIX™

Dark Horse Books

president & publisher **MIKE RICHARDSON**

original collection editor **DIANA SCHUTZ**

second edition editor **DANIEL CHABON**   *assistant editor* **CHUCK HOWITT**

designer **PATRICK SATTERFIELD**   *digital art technician* **ADAM PRUETT**

published by
DARK HORSE BOOKS
a division of Dark Horse Comics LLC
10956 SE Main Street
Milwaukie, OR 97222

DarkHorse.com

To find a comics shop in your area, visit
comicshoplocator.com

First hardcover edition: April 2021
Ebook ISBN: 978-1-50671-685-5
Hardcover ISBN: 978-1-50671-684-8

10 9 8 7 6 5 4 3 2 1
Printed in China

Library of Congress Cataloging-in-Publication Data

Title: Autobiographix.
Description: First hardcover edition. | Milwaukie, OR : Dark Horse Books,
   2021. | Summary: "A premium collection demonstrating the effectiveness
   of the comics medium for telling the most personal of stories-the
   autobiography. Showcasing some of the first published autobiographical
   stories from living-legend artists, mainstream greats, and young "indie"
   up-and-comers!"-- Provided by publisher.
Identifiers: LCCN 2020045068 | ISBN 9781506716848 (hardcover) | ISBN
   9781506716855 (ebook)
Subjects: LCSH: Comic books, strips, etc. | LCGFT: Autobiographical comics
Classification: LCC PN6720 .A88 2021 | DDC 741.5/9 [B]--dc23
LC record available at https://lccn.loc.gov/2020045068

TABLE OF CONTENTS

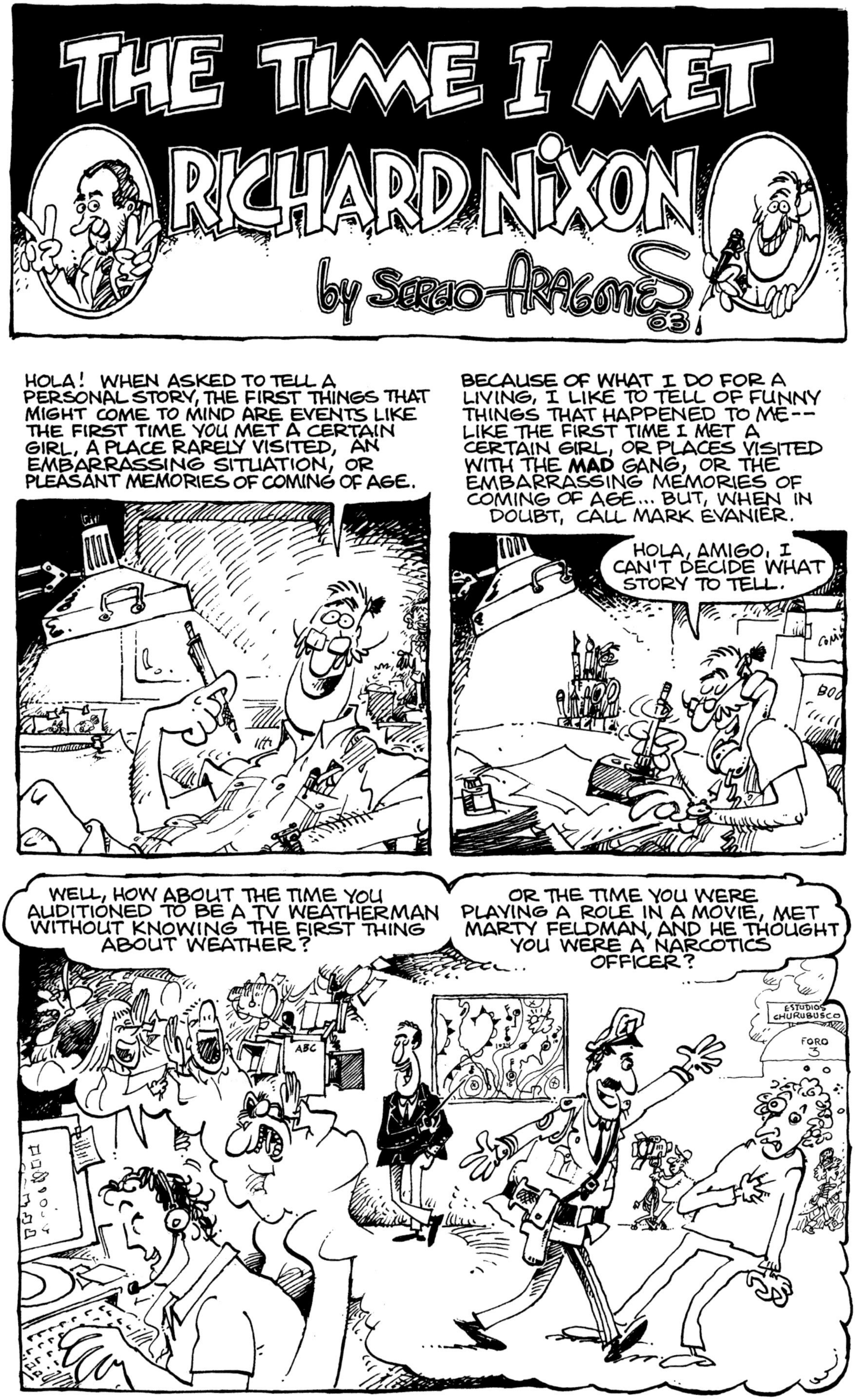
THE TIME I MET RICHARD NIXON
by SERGIO ARAGONÉS '03
HOLA! WHEN ASKED TO TELL A PERSONAL STORY, THE FIRST THINGS THAT MIGHT COME TO MIND ARE EVENTS LIKE THE FIRST TIME YOU MET A CERTAIN GIRL, A PLACE RARELY VISITED, AN EMBARRASSING SITUATION, OR PLEASANT MEMORIES OF COMING OF AGE.
BECAUSE OF WHAT I DO FOR A LIVING, I LIKE TO TELL OF FUNNY THINGS THAT HAPPENED TO ME-- LIKE THE FIRST TIME I MET A CERTAIN GIRL, OR PLACES VISITED WITH THE MAD GANG, OR THE EMBARRASSING MEMORIES OF COMING OF AGE... BUT, WHEN IN DOUBT, CALL MARK EVANIER.
HOLA, AMIGO, I CAN'T DECIDE WHAT STORY TO TELL.
WELL, HOW ABOUT THE TIME YOU AUDITIONED TO BE A TV WEATHERMAN WITHOUT KNOWING THE FIRST THING ABOUT WEATHER?
OR THE TIME YOU WERE PLAYING A ROLE IN A MOVIE, MET MARTY FELDMAN, AND HE THOUGHT YOU WERE A NARCOTICS OFFICER?
ABC
ESTUDIOS CHURUBUSCO
FORO 3

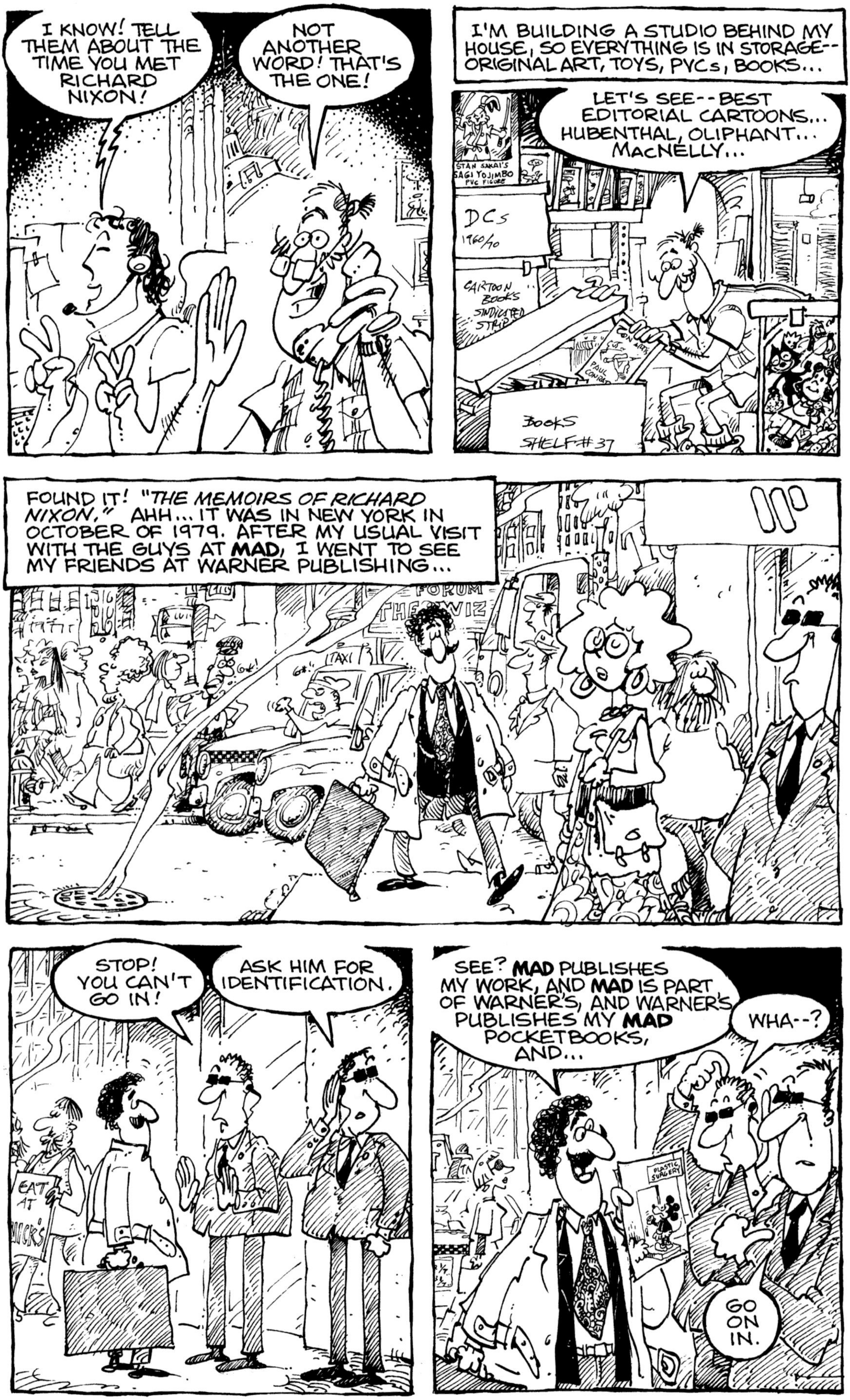
I KNOW! TELL THEM ABOUT THE TIME YOU MET RICHARD NIXON!
NOT ANOTHER WORD! THAT'S THE ONE!
I'M BUILDING A STUDIO BEHIND MY HOUSE, SO EVERYTHING IS IN STORAGE--ORIGINAL ART, TOYS, PVCs, BOOKS...
STAN SAKAI'S USAGI YOJIMBO PVC FIGURE
DCs 1960/70
CARTOON BOOKS SYNDICATED STRIPS
LET'S SEE--BEST EDITORIAL CARTOONS... HUBENTHAL, OLIPHANT... MacNELLY...
BOOKS SHELF #37
FOUND IT! *"THE MEMOIRS OF RICHARD NIXON."* AHH... IT WAS IN NEW YORK IN OCTOBER OF 1979. AFTER MY USUAL VISIT WITH THE GUYS AT **MAD**, I WENT TO SEE MY FRIENDS AT WARNER PUBLISHING...
FORUM
THE WIZ
TAXI
STOP! YOU CAN'T GO IN!
ASK HIM FOR IDENTIFICATION.
EAT AT NICK'S
SEE? **MAD** PUBLISHES MY WORK, AND **MAD** IS PART OF WARNER'S, AND WARNER'S PUBLISHES MY **MAD** POCKETBOOKS, AND...
WHA--?
PLASTIC SURGERY
GO ON IN.

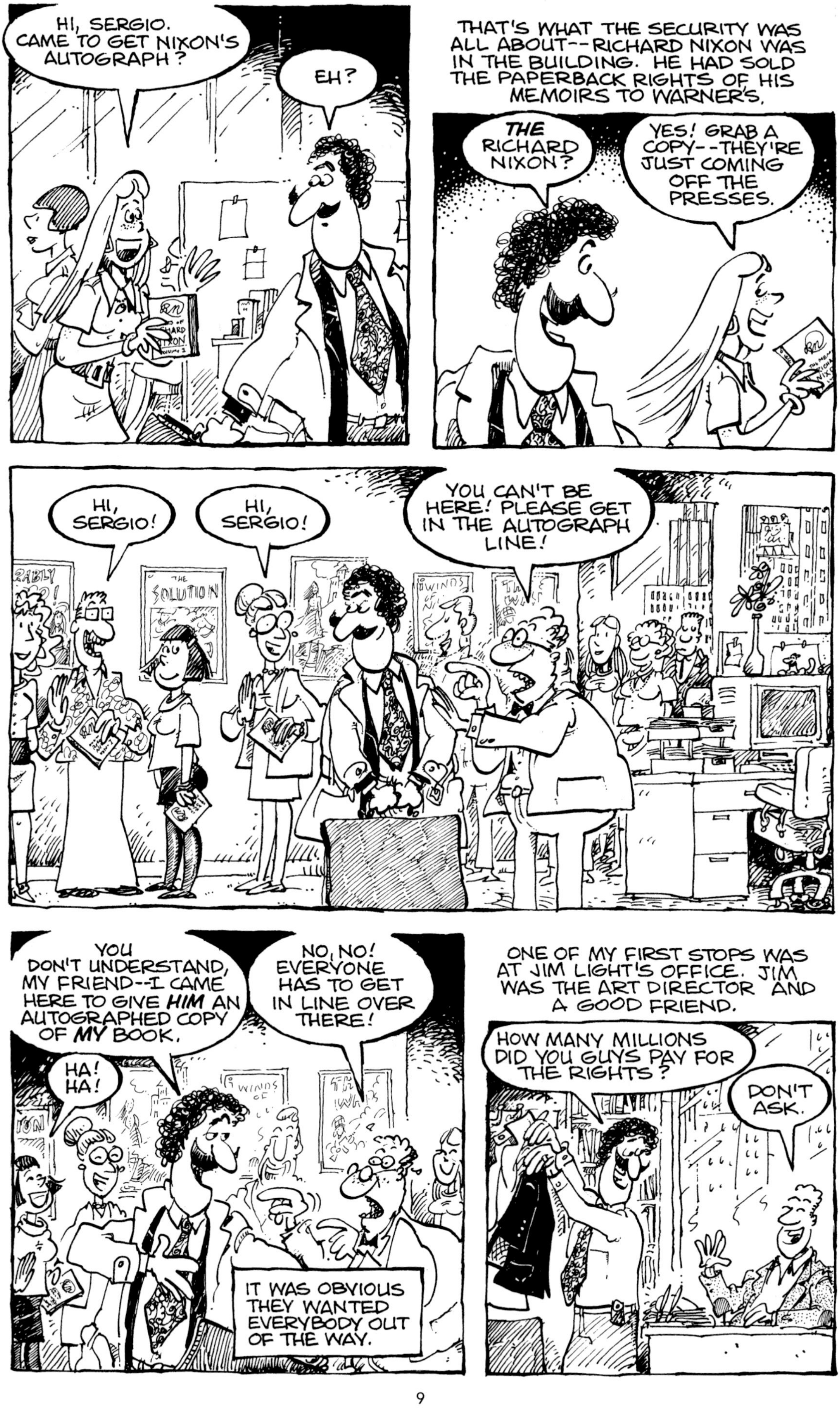

HI, SERGIO. CAME TO GET NIXON'S AUTOGRAPH?
EH?
THAT'S WHAT THE SECURITY WAS ALL ABOUT--RICHARD NIXON WAS IN THE BUILDING. HE HAD SOLD THE PAPERBACK RIGHTS OF HIS MEMOIRS TO WARNER'S.
THE RICHARD NIXON?
YES! GRAB A COPY--THEY'RE JUST COMING OFF THE PRESSES.
HI, SERGIO!
HI, SERGIO!
YOU CAN'T BE HERE! PLEASE GET IN THE AUTOGRAPH LINE!
YOU DON'T UNDERSTAND, MY FRIEND--I CAME HERE TO GIVE *HIM* AN AUTOGRAPHED COPY OF *MY* BOOK.
HA! HA!
NO, NO! EVERYONE HAS TO GET IN LINE OVER THERE!
IT WAS OBVIOUS THEY WANTED EVERYBODY OUT OF THE WAY.
ONE OF MY FIRST STOPS WAS AT JIM LIGHT'S OFFICE. JIM WAS THE ART DIRECTOR AND A GOOD FRIEND.
HOW MANY MILLIONS DID YOU GUYS PAY FOR THE RIGHTS?
DON'T ASK.

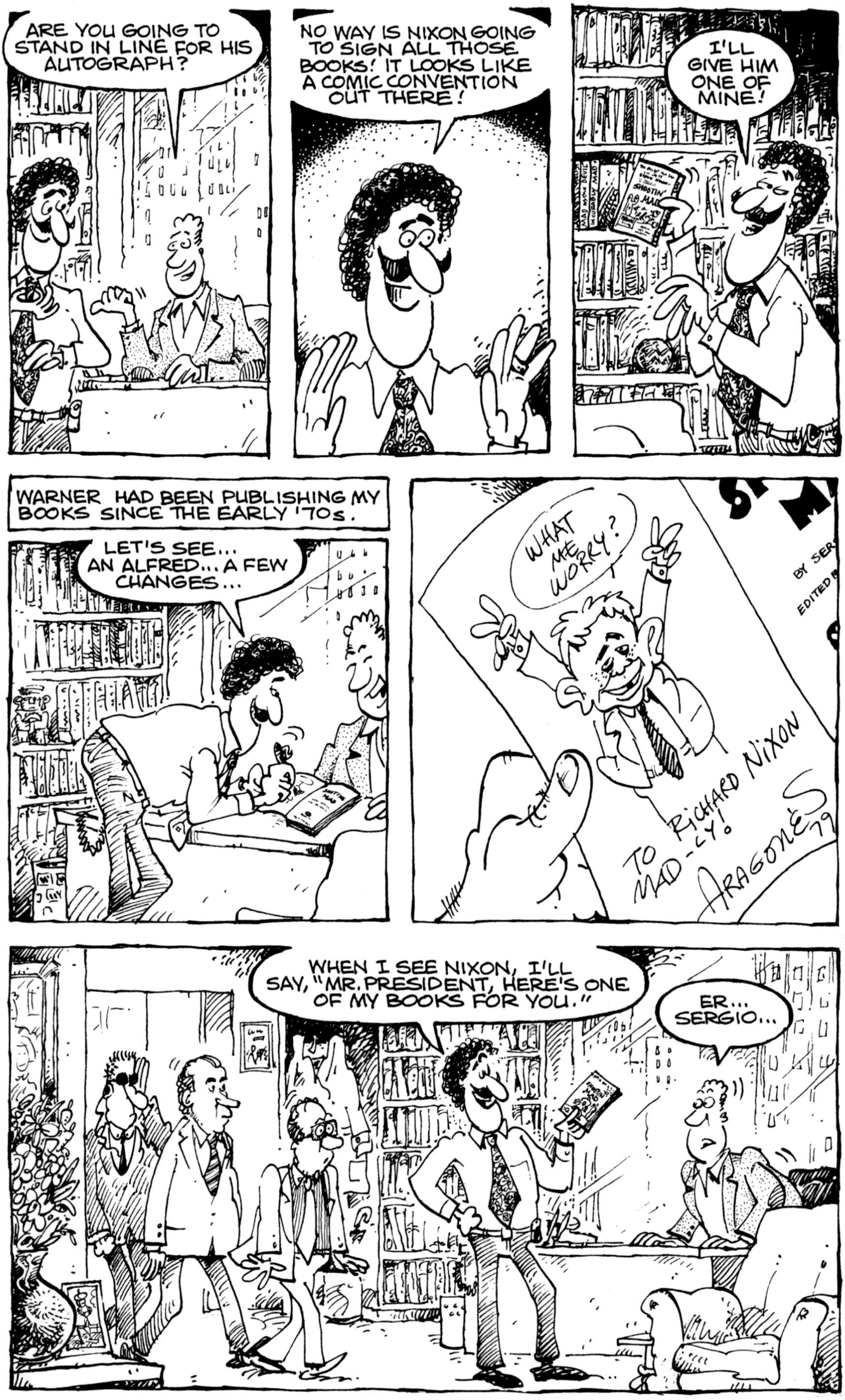
ARE YOU GOING TO STAND IN LINE FOR HIS AUTOGRAPH?
NO WAY IS NIXON GOING TO SIGN ALL THOSE BOOKS! IT LOOKS LIKE A COMIC CONVENTION OUT THERE!
I'LL GIVE HIM ONE OF MINE!
WARNER HAD BEEN PUBLISHING MY BOOKS SINCE THE EARLY '70s.
LET'S SEE... AN ALFRED... A FEW CHANGES...
WHAT ME WORRY?
TO RICHARD NIXON MAD-LY!
ARAGONÉS '79
WHEN I SEE NIXON, I'LL SAY, "MR. PRESIDENT, HERE'S ONE OF MY BOOKS FOR YOU."
ER... SERGIO...

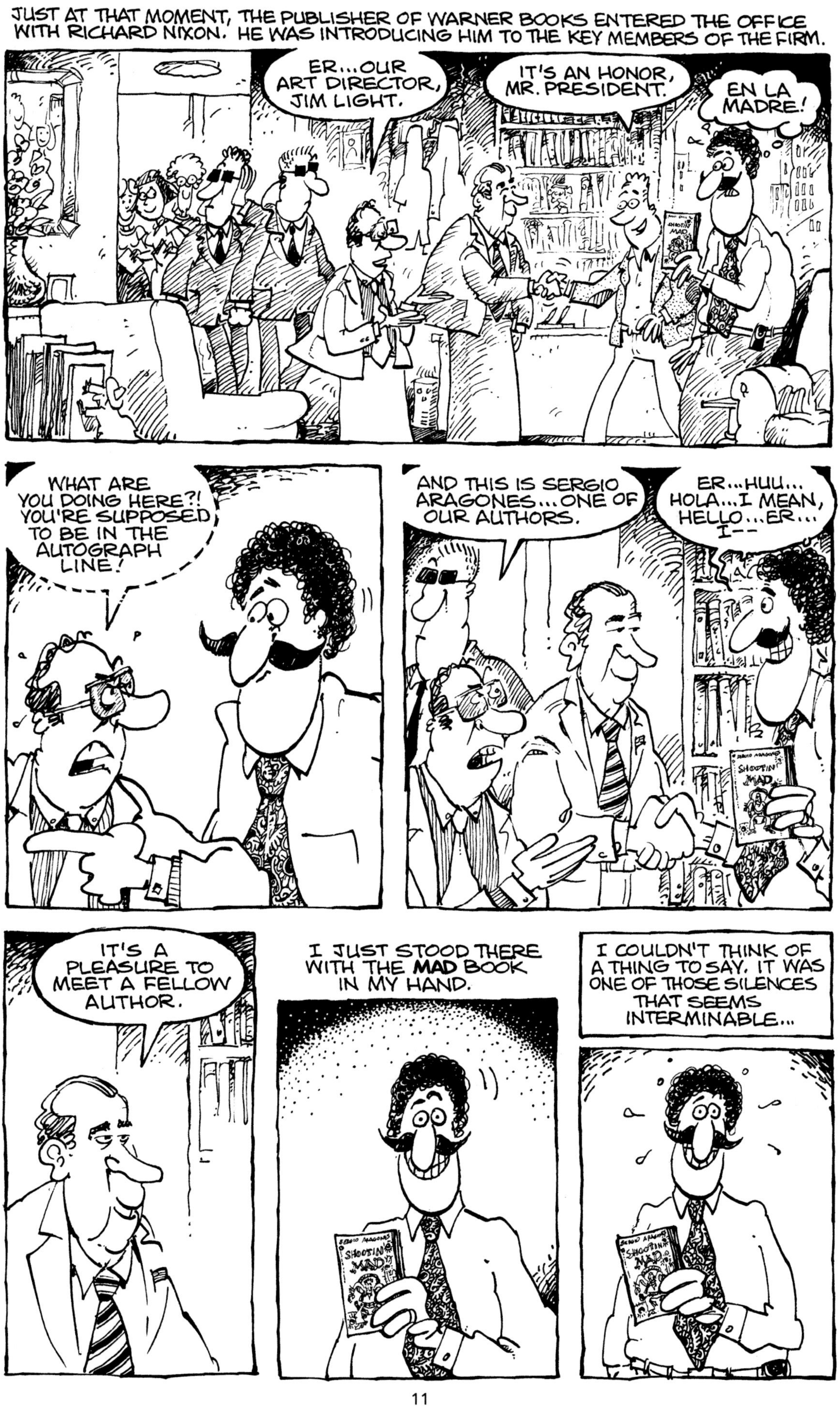

JUST AT THAT MOMENT, THE PUBLISHER OF WARNER BOOKS ENTERED THE OFFICE WITH RICHARD NIXON. HE WAS INTRODUCING HIM TO THE KEY MEMBERS OF THE FIRM.
ER...OUR ART DIRECTOR, JIM LIGHT.
IT'S AN HONOR, MR. PRESIDENT.
EN LA MADRE!
WHAT ARE YOU DOING HERE?! YOU'RE SUPPOSED TO BE IN THE AUTOGRAPH LINE!
AND THIS IS SERGIO ARAGONES...ONE OF OUR AUTHORS.
ER...HUU... HOLA...I MEAN, HELLO...ER... I--
IT'S A PLEASURE TO MEET A FELLOW AUTHOR.
I JUST STOOD THERE WITH THE MAD BOOK IN MY HAND.
I COULDN'T THINK OF A THING TO SAY. IT WAS ONE OF THOSE SILENCES THAT SEEMS INTERMINABLE...

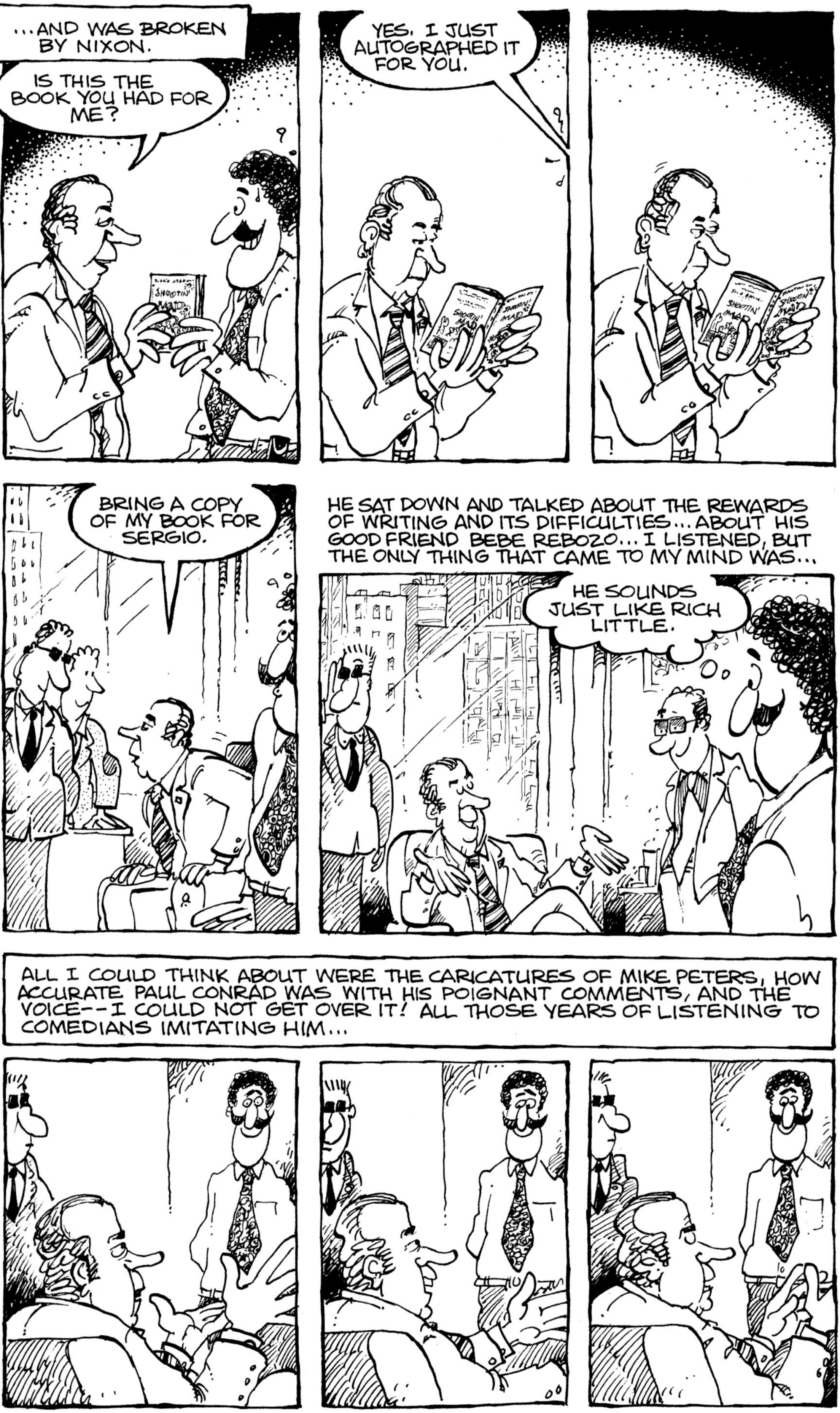

...AND WAS BROKEN BY NIXON.
IS THIS THE BOOK YOU HAD FOR ME?
YES. I JUST AUTOGRAPHED IT FOR YOU.
SHOOTIN' MAD
BRING A COPY OF MY BOOK FOR SERGIO.
HE SAT DOWN AND TALKED ABOUT THE REWARDS OF WRITING AND ITS DIFFICULTIES... ABOUT HIS GOOD FRIEND BEBE REBOZO... I LISTENED, BUT THE ONLY THING THAT CAME TO MY MIND WAS...
HE SOUNDS JUST LIKE RICH LITTLE.
ALL I COULD THINK ABOUT WERE THE CARICATURES OF MIKE PETERS, HOW ACCURATE PAUL CONRAD WAS WITH HIS POIGNANT COMMENTS, AND THE VOICE--I COULD NOT GET OVER IT! ALL THOSE YEARS OF LISTENING TO COMEDIANS IMITATING HIM...

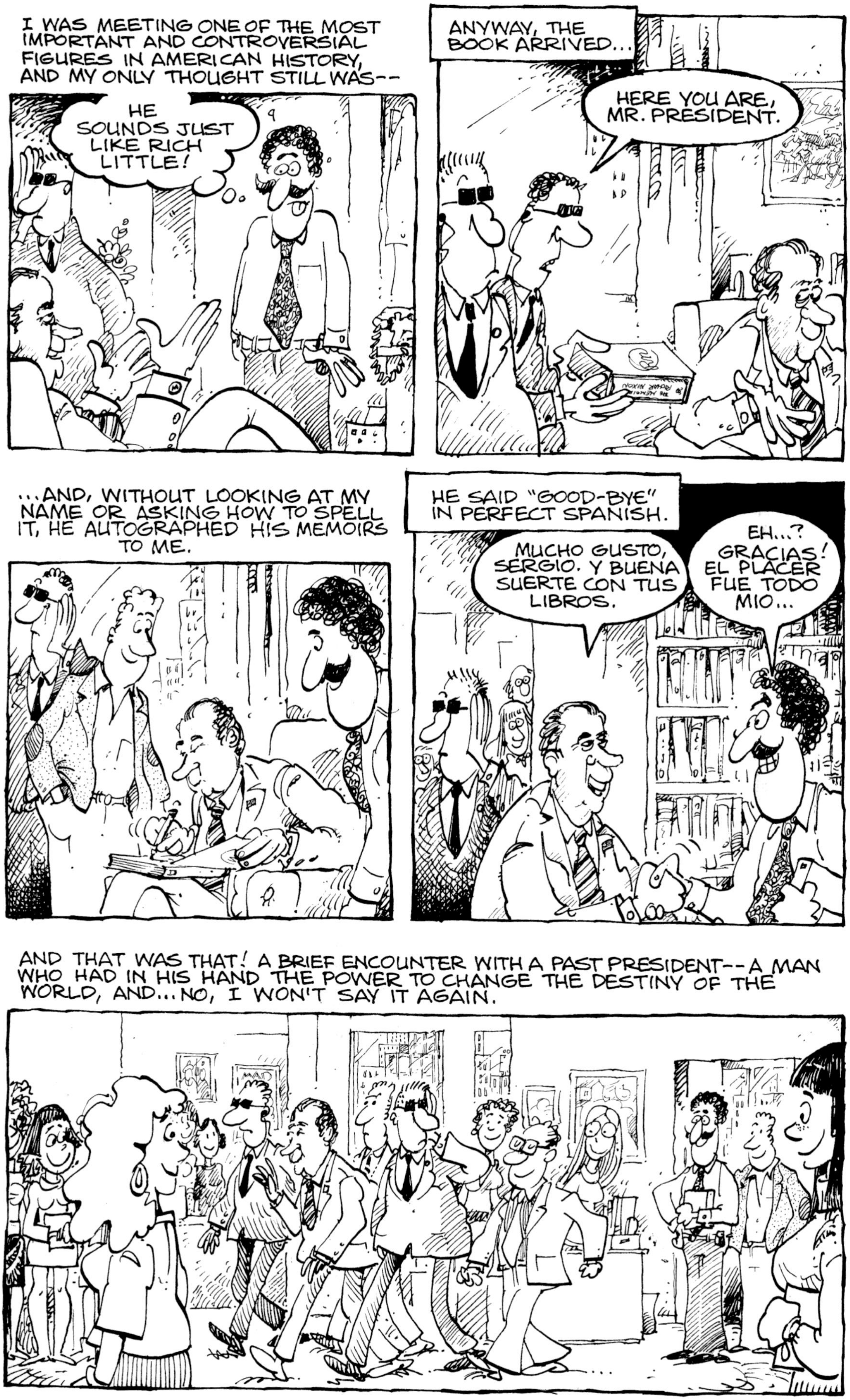
I WAS MEETING ONE OF THE MOST IMPORTANT AND CONTROVERSIAL FIGURES IN AMERICAN HISTORY, AND MY ONLY THOUGHT STILL WAS--
HE SOUNDS JUST LIKE RICH LITTLE!
ANYWAY, THE BOOK ARRIVED...
HERE YOU ARE, MR. PRESIDENT.
...AND, WITHOUT LOOKING AT MY NAME OR ASKING HOW TO SPELL IT, HE AUTOGRAPHED HIS MEMOIRS TO ME.
HE SAID "GOOD-BYE" IN PERFECT SPANISH.
MUCHO GUSTO, SERGIO. Y BUENA SUERTE CON TUS LIBROS.
EH...? GRACIAS! EL PLACER FUE TODO MIO...
AND THAT WAS THAT! A BRIEF ENCOUNTER WITH A PAST PRESIDENT--A MAN WHO HAD IN HIS HAND THE POWER TO CHANGE THE DESTINY OF THE WORLD, AND...NO, I WON'T SAY IT AGAIN.

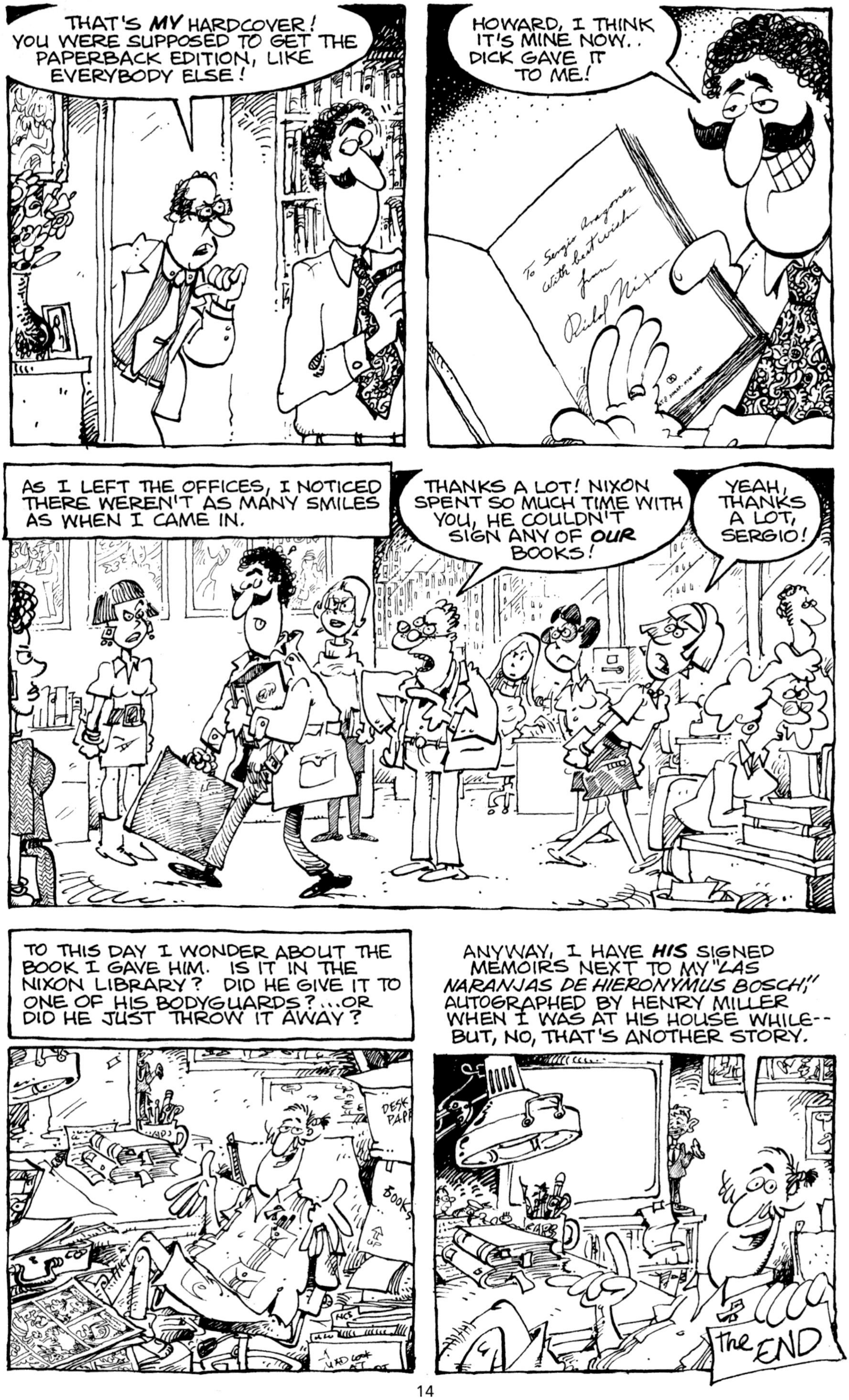
THAT'S MY HARDCOVER! YOU WERE SUPPOSED TO GET THE PAPERBACK EDITION, LIKE EVERYBODY ELSE!
HOWARD, I THINK IT'S MINE NOW. DICK GAVE IT TO ME!
To Sergio Aragones With best wishes from Richard Nixon
AS I LEFT THE OFFICES, I NOTICED THERE WEREN'T AS MANY SMILES AS WHEN I CAME IN.
THANKS A LOT! NIXON SPENT SO MUCH TIME WITH YOU, HE COULDN'T SIGN ANY OF OUR BOOKS!
YEAH, THANKS A LOT, SERGIO!
TO THIS DAY I WONDER ABOUT THE BOOK I GAVE HIM. IS IT IN THE NIXON LIBRARY? DID HE GIVE IT TO ONE OF HIS BODYGUARDS?...OR DID HE JUST THROW IT AWAY?
ANYWAY, I HAVE HIS SIGNED MEMOIRS NEXT TO MY "LAS NARANJAS DE HIERONYMUS BOSCH," AUTOGRAPHED BY HENRY MILLER WHEN I WAS AT HIS HOUSE WHILE-- BUT, NO, THAT'S ANOTHER STORY.
BOOKS
The END

THE DAY I BECAME A PROFESSIONAL

BY Will Eisner

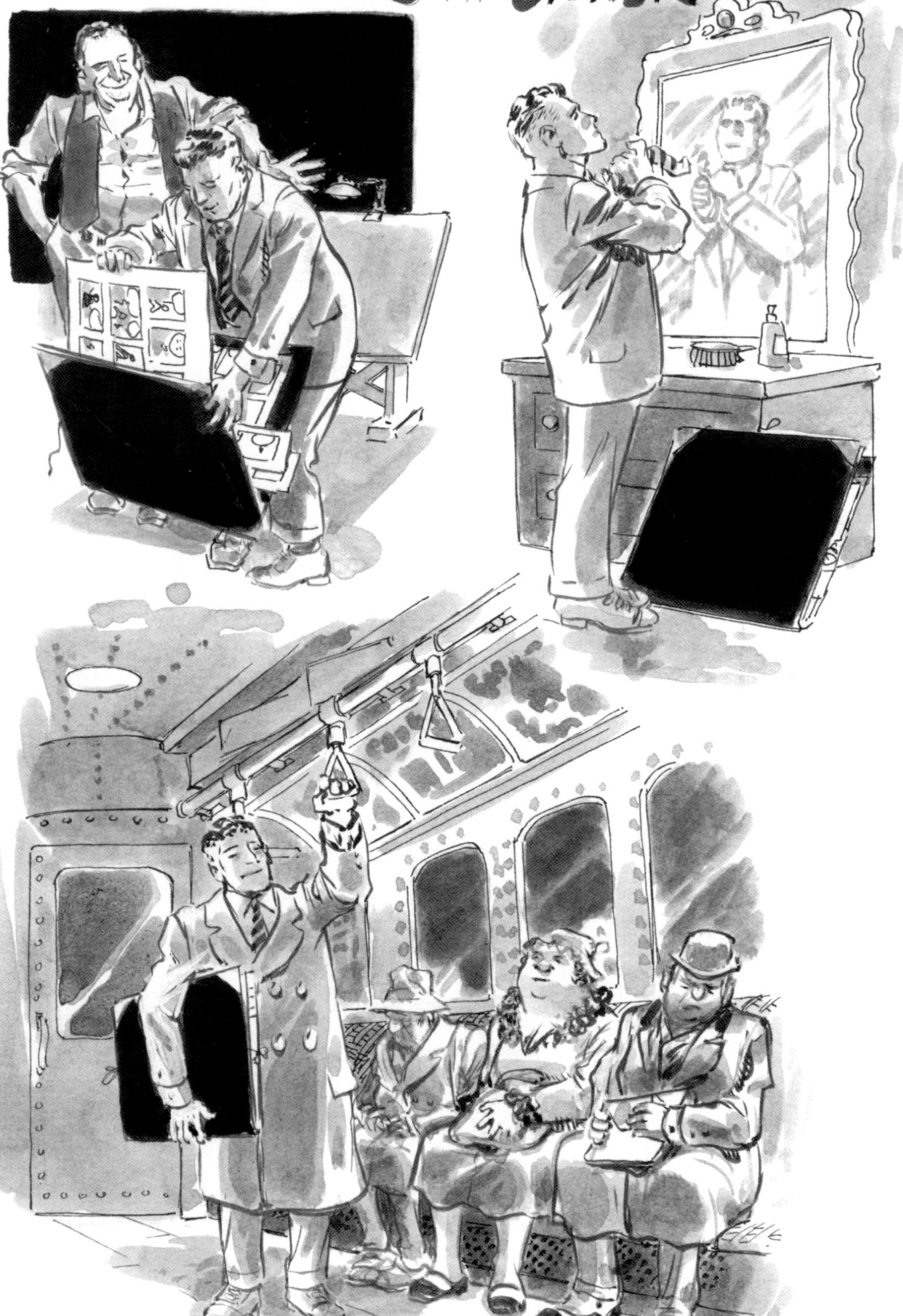

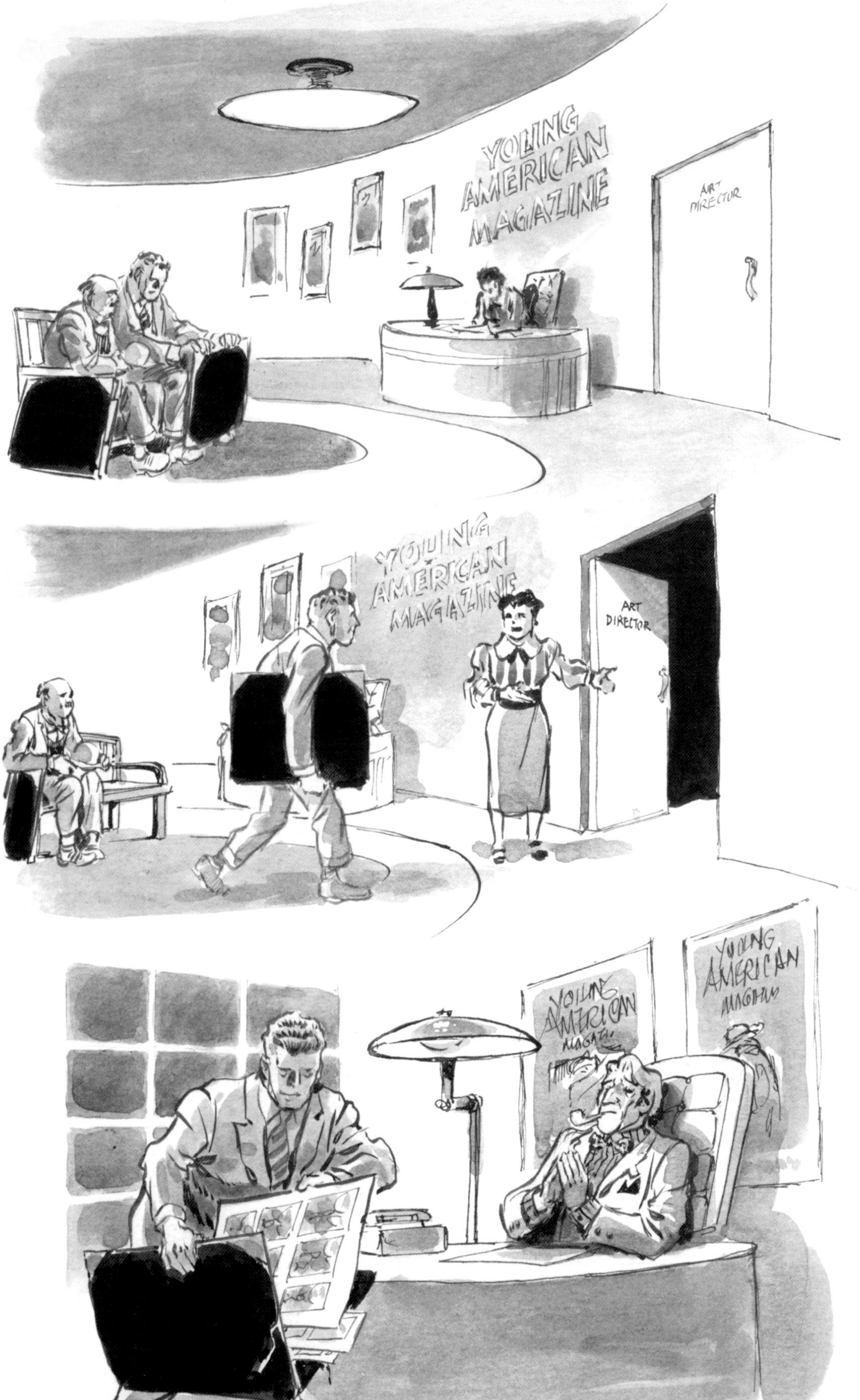
YOUNG AMERICAN MAGAZINE
ART DIRECTOR
YOUNG AMERICAN MAGAZINE
ART DIRECTOR
YOUNG AMERICAN
YOUNG AMERICAN

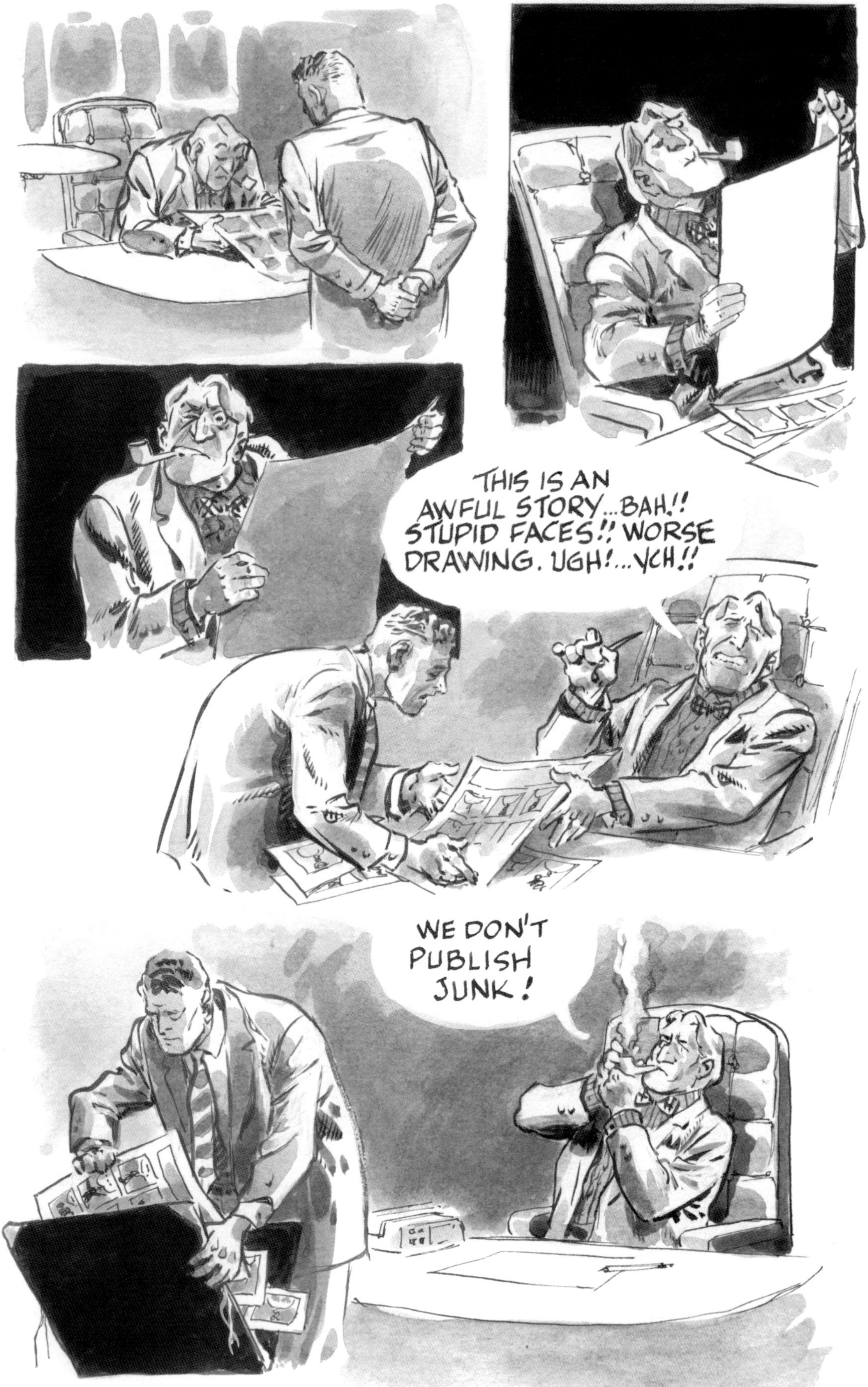
THIS IS AN AWFUL STORY...BAH!! STUPID FACES!! WORSE DRAWING. UGH!...YCH!!
WE DON'T PUBLISH JUNK!

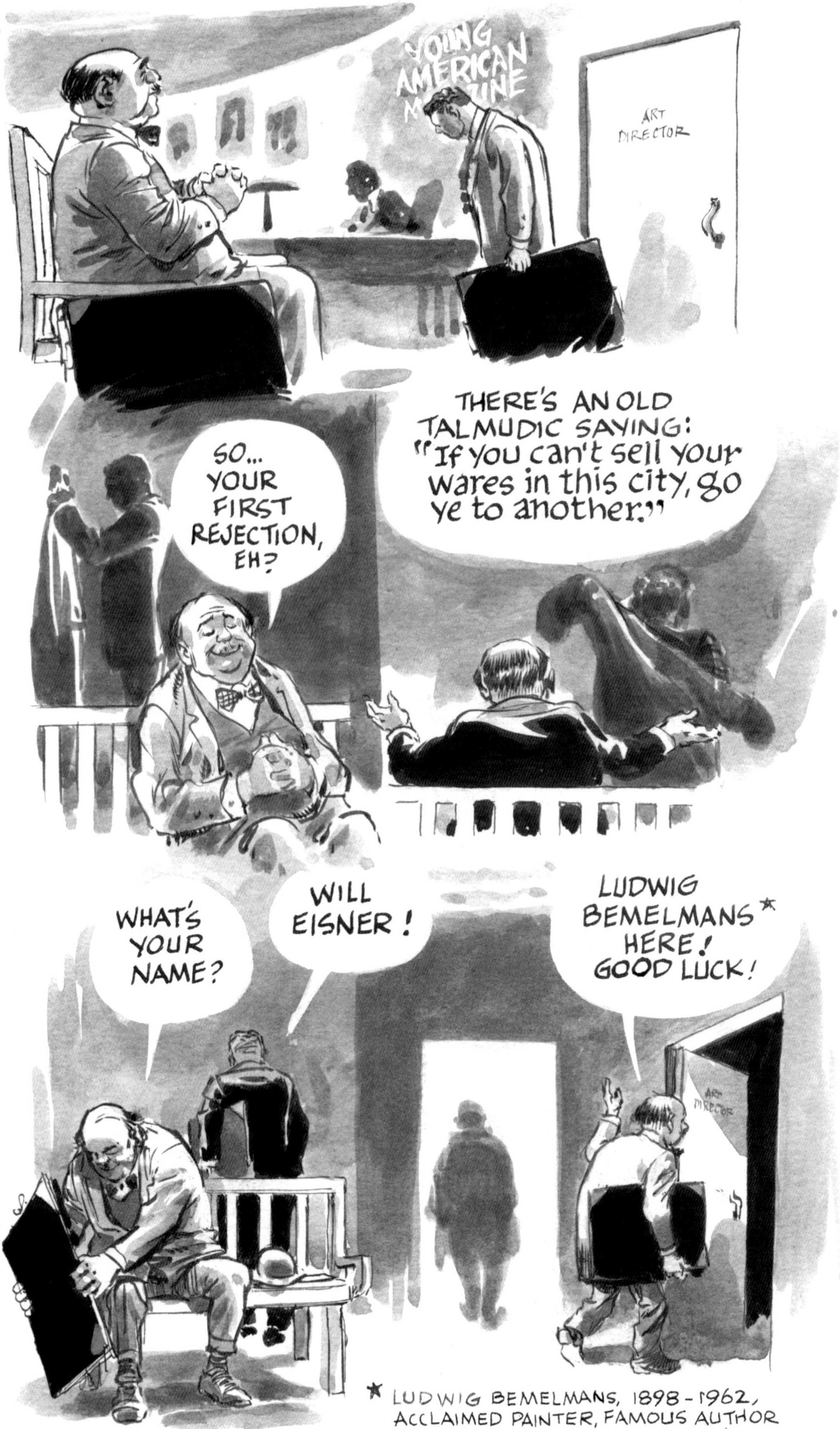
YOUNG AMERICAN
ART DIRECTOR
SO... YOUR FIRST REJECTION, EH?
THERE'S AN OLD TALMUDIC SAYING: "If you can't sell your wares in this city, go ye to another."
WHAT'S YOUR NAME?
WILL EISNER!
LUDWIG BEMELMANS* HERE! GOOD LUCK!
ART DIRECTOR

* LUDWIG BEMELMANS, 1898-1962, ACCLAIMED PAINTER, FAMOUS AUTHOR AND ILLUSTRATOR OF CHILDREN'S BOOKS

RULES *to* LIVE BY
JASON LUTES

When you've lived in one place longer than anywhere else:

leave.

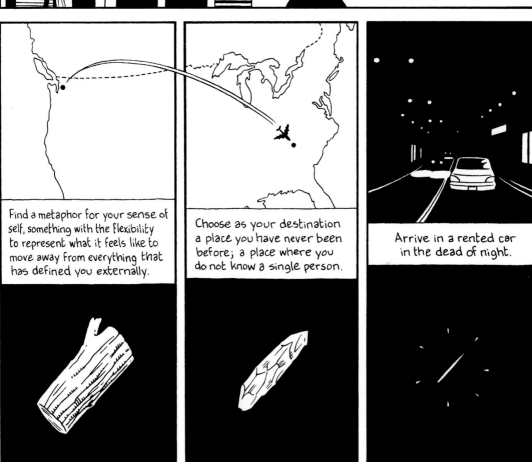

Find a metaphor for your sense of self, something with the flexibility to represent what it feels like to move away from everything that has defined you externally.

Choose as your destination a place you have never been before; a place where you do not know a single person.

Arrive in a rented car in the dead of night.

Stay in a succession of cheap motels, each one worse than the last, while you look for an apartment.

No phones.

Racist manager.

Too secure.

Take the first one-bedroom you can find that rents for under $500 a month, as long as it's on a quiet street within walking distance of downtown.

Private side entrance a plus

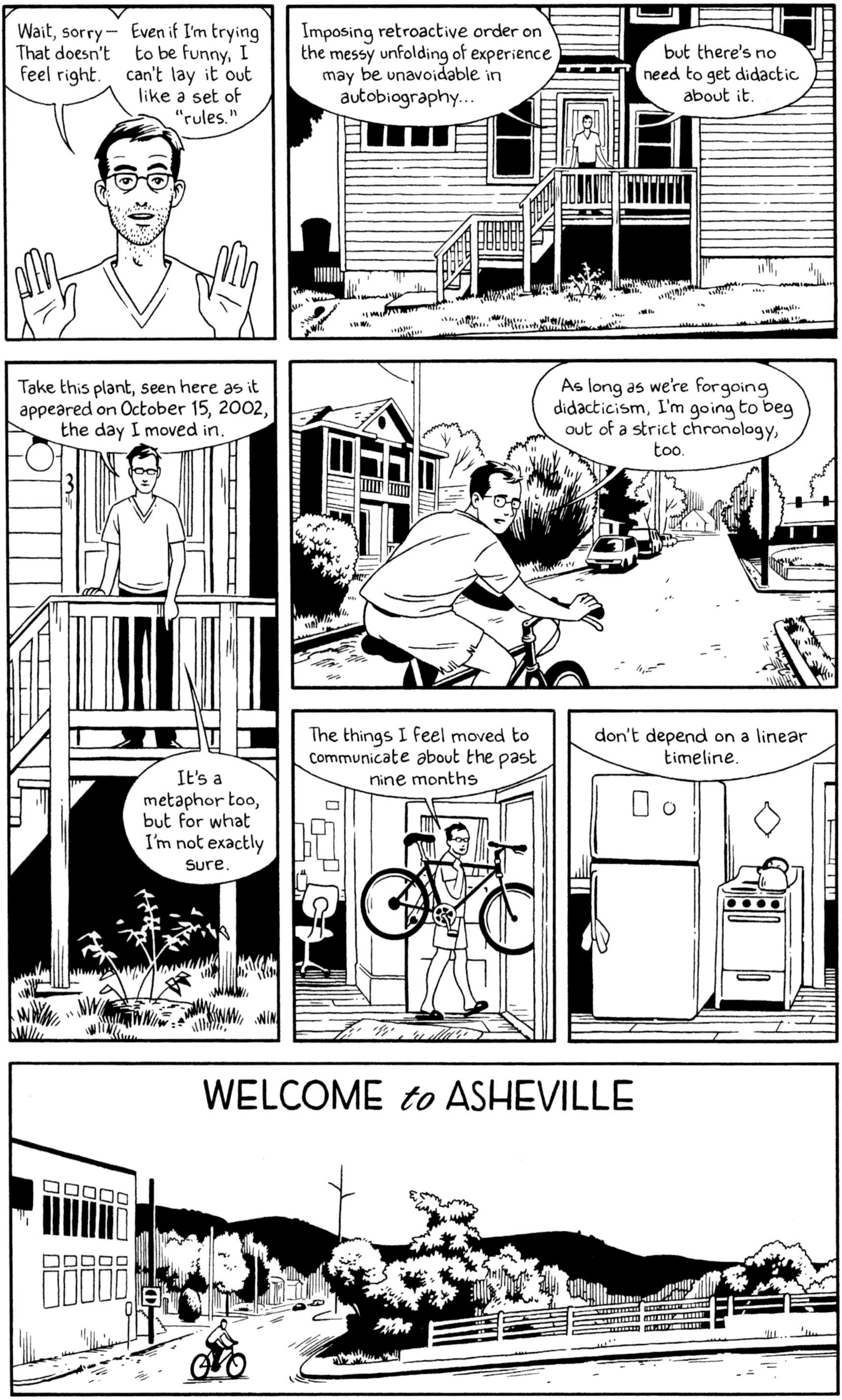
Wait, sorry— That doesn't feel right.
Even if I'm trying to be funny, I can't lay it out like a set of "rules."
Imposing retroactive order on the messy unfolding of experience may be unavoidable in autobiography...
but there's no need to get didactic about it.
Take this plant, seen here as it appeared on October 15, 2002, the day I moved in.
3
It's a metaphor too, but for what I'm not exactly sure.
As long as we're forgoing didacticism, I'm going to beg out of a strict chronology, too.
The things I feel moved to communicate about the past nine months
don't depend on a linear timeline.
WELCOME to ASHEVILLE

A "sense of place" in a story is important to me.

I think that your environment can be as much a part of you as you are a part of it.

But only if you let it.

Living here, getting around only on foot or by bike, has made me feel that all the more acutely.

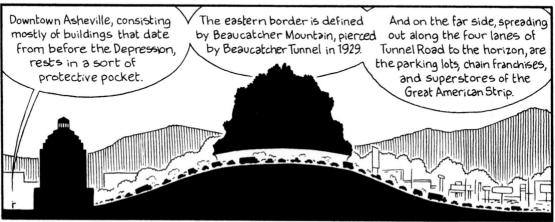

Downtown Asheville, consisting mostly of buildings that date from before the Depression, rests in a sort of protective pocket.

The eastern border is defined by Beaucatcher Mountain, pierced by Beaucatcher Tunnel in 1929.

And on the far side, spreading out along the four lanes of Tunnel Road to the horizon, are the parking lots, chain franchises, and superstores of the Great American Strip.

Walking from downtown out to Tunnel Road is dispiriting, to say the least. The Tunnel was not built for pedestrians, and the traffic is deafening.

The first time I did it, to buy a cheese grater at Wal-Mart, it felt like my own personal descent into Hell.

I tried to see the experience in symbolic terms, to relate it to the fragile state of my psyche, but in the end I had to question the whole idea of using landscape to *represent* something.

THIS *is not a* METAPHOR

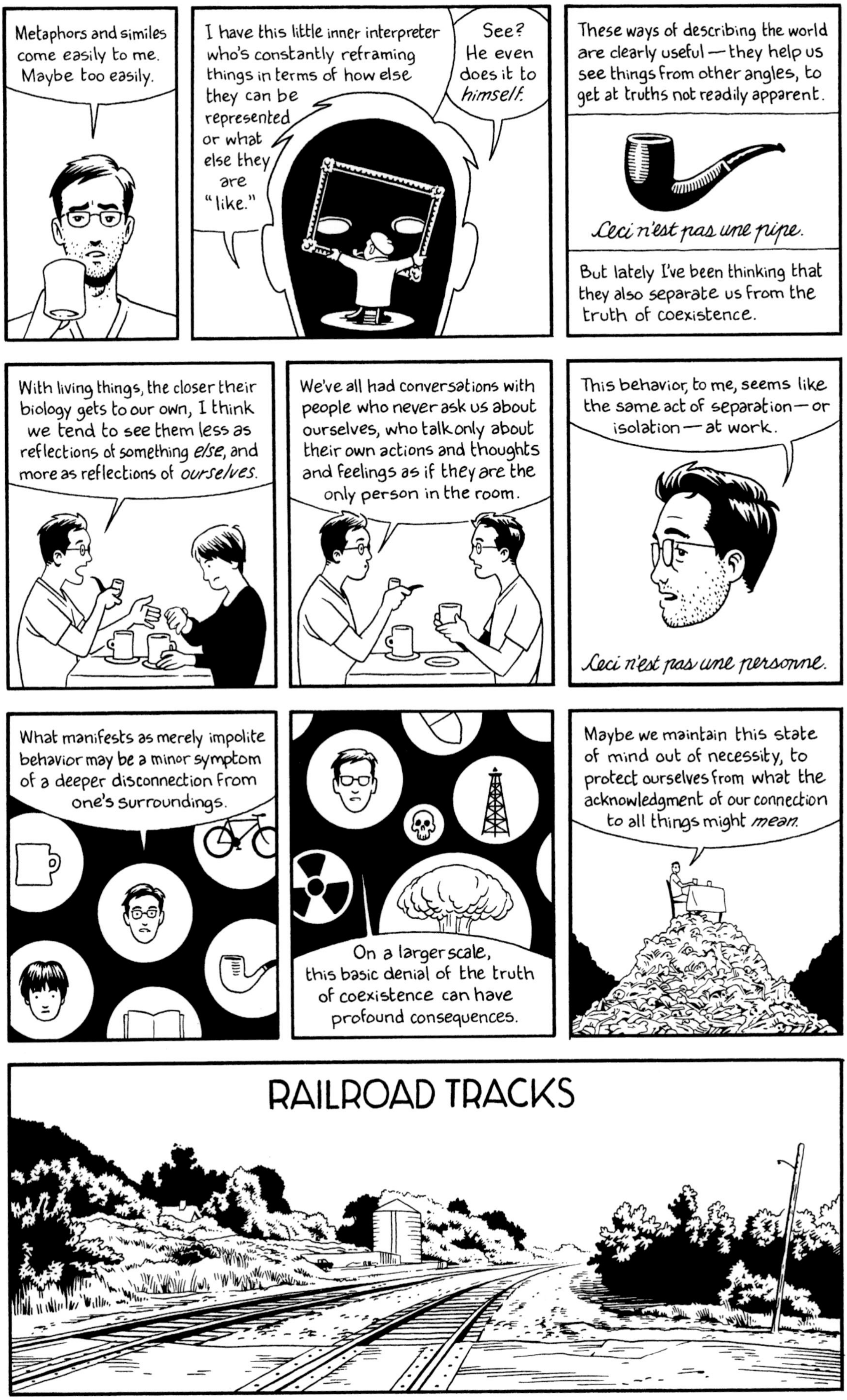
Metaphors and similes come easily to me. Maybe too easily.
I have this little inner interpreter who's constantly reframing things in terms of how else they can be represented or what else they are "like."
See? He even does it to *himself.*
These ways of describing the world are clearly useful — they help us see things from other angles, to get at truths not readily apparent.
Ceci n'est pas une pipe.
But lately I've been thinking that they also separate us from the truth of coexistence.
With living things, the closer their biology gets to our own, I think we tend to see them less as reflections of something *else*, and more as reflections of *ourselves*.
We've all had conversations with people who never ask us about ourselves, who talk only about their own actions and thoughts and feelings as if they are the only person in the room.
This behavior, to me, seems like the same act of separation — or isolation — at work.
Ceci n'est pas une personne.
What manifests as merely impolite behavior may be a minor symptom of a deeper disconnection from one's surroundings.
On a larger scale, this basic denial of the truth of coexistence can have profound consequences.
Maybe we maintain this state of mind out of necessity, to protect ourselves from what the acknowledgment of our connection to all things might *mean*.
RAILROAD TRACKS

On February 2, 1966, Cleve Backster made a discovery about this basic disconnection that changed his life.

Mr. Backster is a leading polygraph expert. He created the standard test used by lie detection examiners worldwide, and along with running a lab devoted to polygraph science, he trains law enforcement officials in proper use of the device.

On February 2, 1966, he bought a plant for the lab and, after watering it, decided on a whim to see if a polygraph machine attached to the plant would register any change when the water traveled all the way out to the leaves.

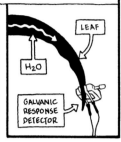

LEAF

H_2O

GALVANIC RESPONSE DETECTOR

He was surprised to see something on the chart resembling a human response, and began to wonder if there might be a way to trigger a physiological response in the plant *that* the polygraph could measure.

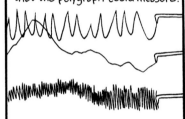

At 13 minutes, 55 seconds chart time, the imagery entered my mind of burning the leaf.

I didn't verbalize, I didn't touch the plant; I didn't touch the equipment.

The pen jumped right off the top of the chart.

This event altered Mr. Backster's consciousness permanently. From that moment on, he devoted his life to studying the extent and ramifications of what some have termed "biocommunication."

Decades of research have led him to believe that, given time, living things can attune themselves to their environment and everything in it, particularly other living things.

He has proven that subjects —plants, yogurt cultures, human cells— register a physiological response when the things to which they are attuned suffer damage, death, or emotional duress.

Instantaneously, at distances of up to 300 miles.

Extrasensory perception?

Primary perception.

a RIVER

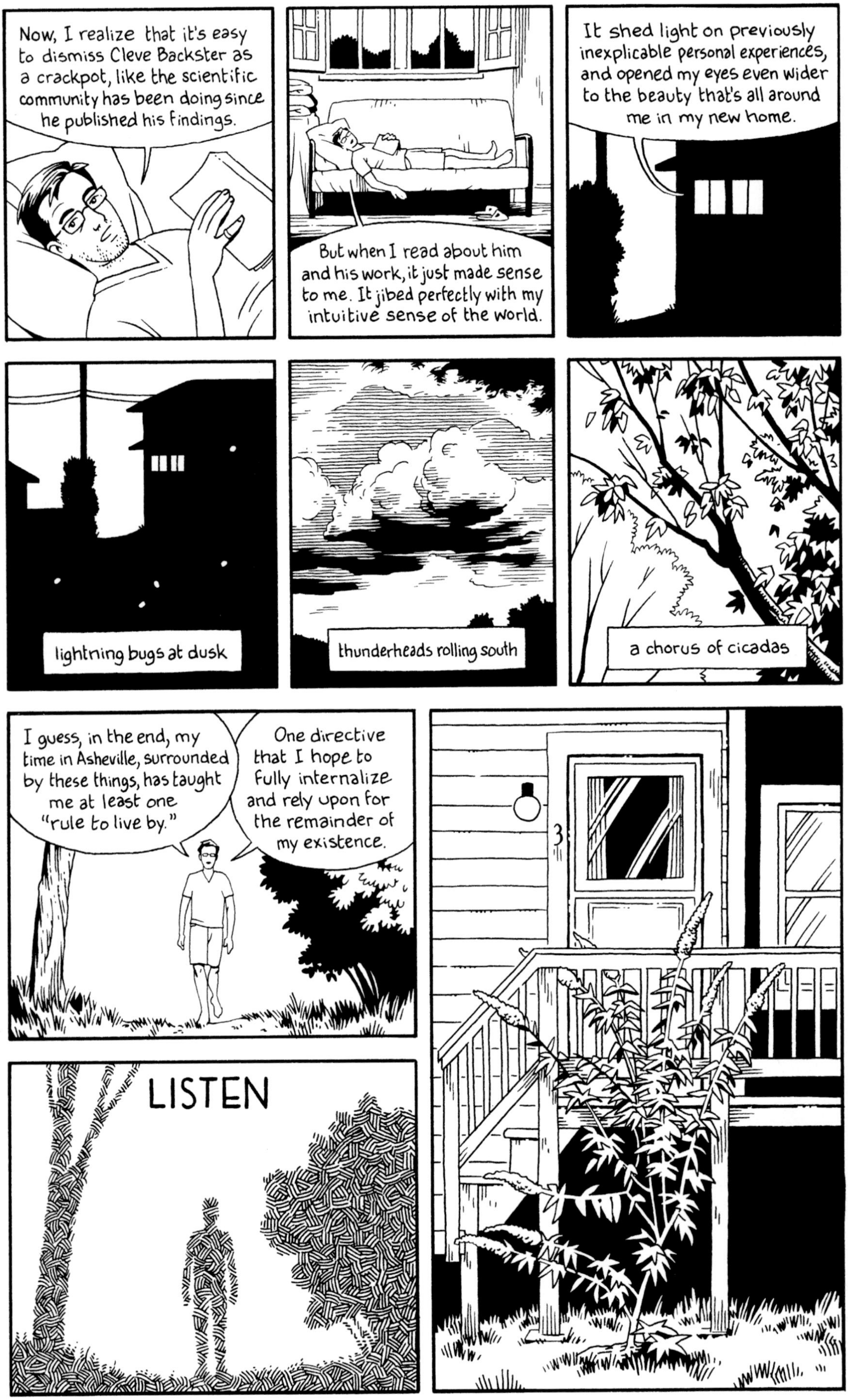
Now, I realize that it's easy to dismiss Cleve Backster as a crackpot, like the scientific community has been doing since he published his findings.
But when I read about him and his work, it just made sense to me. It jibed perfectly with my intuitive sense of the world.
It shed light on previously inexplicable personal experiences, and opened my eyes even wider to the beauty that's all around me in my new home.
lightning bugs at dusk
thunderheads rolling south
a chorus of cicadas
I guess, in the end, my time in Asheville, surrounded by these things, has taught me at least one "rule to live by."
One directive that I hope to fully internalize and rely upon for the remainder of my existence.
3
LISTEN

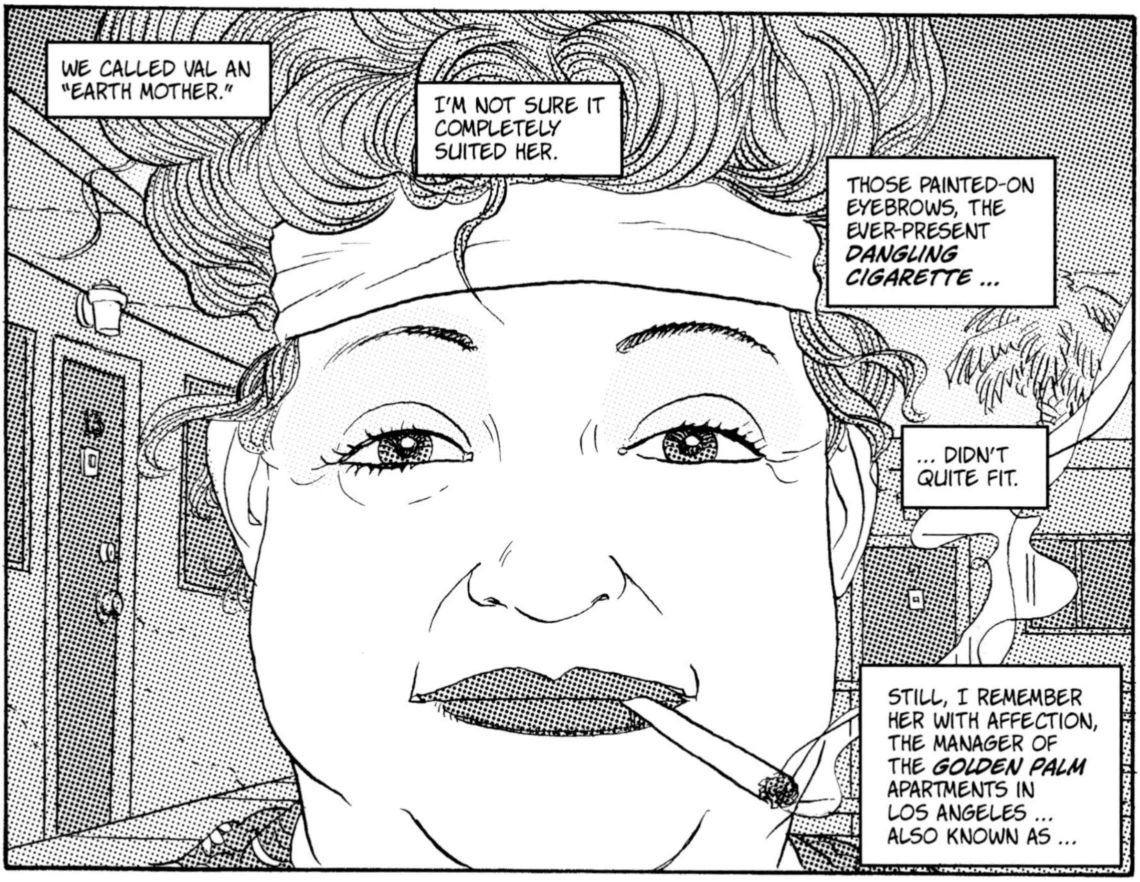
WE CALLED VAL AN "EARTH MOTHER."
I'M NOT SURE IT COMPLETELY SUITED HER.
THOSE PAINTED-ON EYEBROWS, THE EVER-PRESENT DANGLING CIGARETTE ...
... DIDN'T QUITE FIT.
STILL, I REMEMBER HER WITH AFFECTION, THE MANAGER OF THE GOLDEN PALM APARTMENTS IN LOS ANGELES ... ALSO KNOWN AS ...

THE BUILDING THAT DIDN'T EXPLODE

PAUL CHADWICK 2003

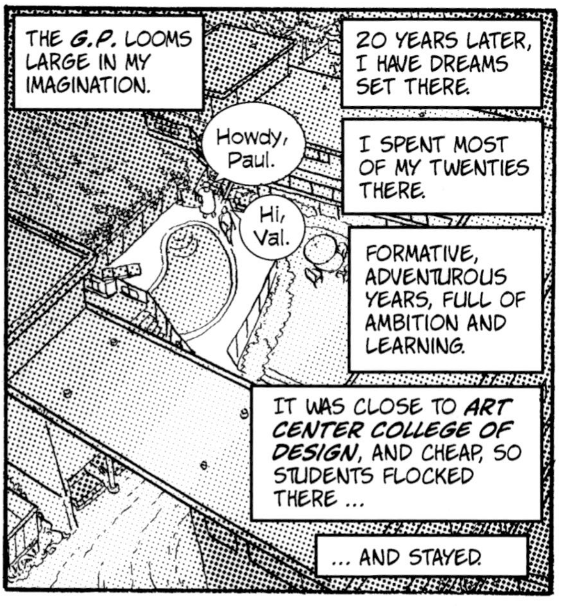
THE G.P. LOOMS LARGE IN MY IMAGINATION.
20 YEARS LATER, I HAVE DREAMS SET THERE.
Howdy, Paul.
Hi, Val.
I SPENT MOST OF MY TWENTIES THERE.
FORMATIVE, ADVENTUROUS YEARS, FULL OF AMBITION AND LEARNING.
IT WAS CLOSE TO ART CENTER COLLEGE OF DESIGN, AND CHEAP, SO STUDENTS FLOCKED THERE ...
... AND STAYED.

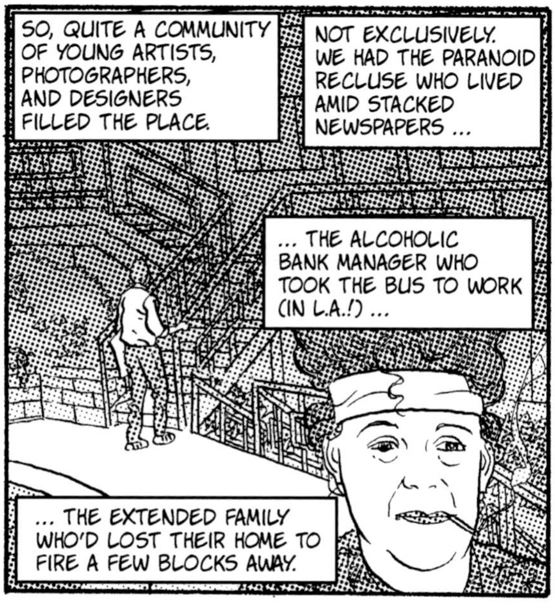
SO, QUITE A COMMUNITY OF YOUNG ARTISTS, PHOTOGRAPHERS, AND DESIGNERS FILLED THE PLACE.
NOT EXCLUSIVELY. WE HAD THE PARANOID RECLUSE WHO LIVED AMID STACKED NEWSPAPERS ...
... THE ALCOHOLIC BANK MANAGER WHO TOOK THE BUS TO WORK (IN L.A.!) ...
... THE EXTENDED FAMILY WHO'D LOST THEIR HOME TO FIRE A FEW BLOCKS AWAY.

COLORFUL PLACE, ALL RIGHT.

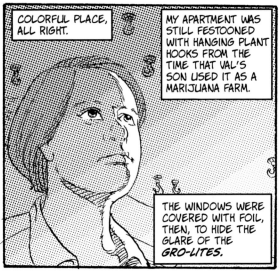

MY APARTMENT WAS STILL FESTOONED WITH HANGING PLANT HOOKS FROM THE TIME THAT VAL'S SON USED IT AS A MARIJUANA FARM.

THE WINDOWS WERE COVERED WITH FOIL, THEN, TO HIDE THE GLARE OF THE *GRO-LITES.*

BUT WHAT WAS SPECIAL ABOUT THE PLACE WAS ITS CONCENTRATION OF TALENTED YOUNG PEOPLE WHO WENT ON TO MAKE A MARK.

I added a hook or two, too!

THE *G.P.* WAS A LAUNCH PAD FOR A LOT OF CAREERS.

BY MY COUNT I WENT THROUGH SEVEN ROOMMATES IN MY ART CENTER YEARS AND AFTER.

HMM. WAS I *THAT* HARD TO LIVE WITH?

NOT REALLY. PEOPLE THAT AGE MOVE FREQUENTLY.

THE FIRST, AN ENDURING FRIEND, WAS DAVE MATTINGLY, SOON TO BECOME ONE OF THE LEADING *SF* ARTISTS.

TOM KINKADE, THE FAMOUS PAINTER OF LIGHT™, FOLLOWED ...

This'll be total blowaway-manship, Chadwick!

... THOUGH THEN HE WAS A HUMBLE BOHEMIAN ART STUDENT. OKAY, MAYBE NOT HUMBLE, EXACTLY.

AND RON HARRIS ... WHO SIMULTANEOUSLY, AND MISERABLY (FOR THE SYNDICATE PEOPLE WERE TRUE JERKS), DREW THE *DALLAS* AND *STAR TREK* NEWSPAPER STRIPS.

They said Charlene Tilton wasn't "pretty enough"!

white paint

BUT THEN HE DID HIS TOTALLY GREAT *CRASH RYAN* RETRO-AVIATION STRIP FOR *EPIC COMICS.*

AND KURT CYRUS ... NOW A TOP-RANK CHILDREN'S BOOK ILLUSTRATOR, THEN A STARVING GENIUS.

sigh ...

My God! That's *BEAUTIFUL!*

I MEAN *STARVING* ... POOR KURT SUPPED EVERY NIGHT ON RICE, PEAS, AND POTATOES, BOILED TOGETHER.

LATER: MARK VERHEIDEN, AUTHOR OF *THE AMERICAN* COMICS SERIES AND *THE MASK* AND *TIME COP* FILMS, NOW BIGWIG ON *SMALLVILLE.*

Quiet. He's writing.

Day job at *L.A. Times* Classifieds.

His "American Grafitti," never filmed, titled *The Big Party.*

His last typewriter.

TWO DOORS DOWN LIVED BRYN BARNARD, ILLUSTRATOR, WRITER, INTERNATIONALIST.

Ada udang dibalik batu.

Even then, he spoke Malay!

A California kid!

AT THIS WRITING, HIS BOOK *DANGEROUS PLANET* HAS JUST BEEN PUBLISHED.

HIS ROOMMATE: JIM GURNEY, WHO'D LATER ENCHANT MILLIONS WITH HIS *DINOTOPIA* BOOKS.

These animal studies will show, I hope, an aptitude for animation drawing.

Rejected by Disney, the fools!

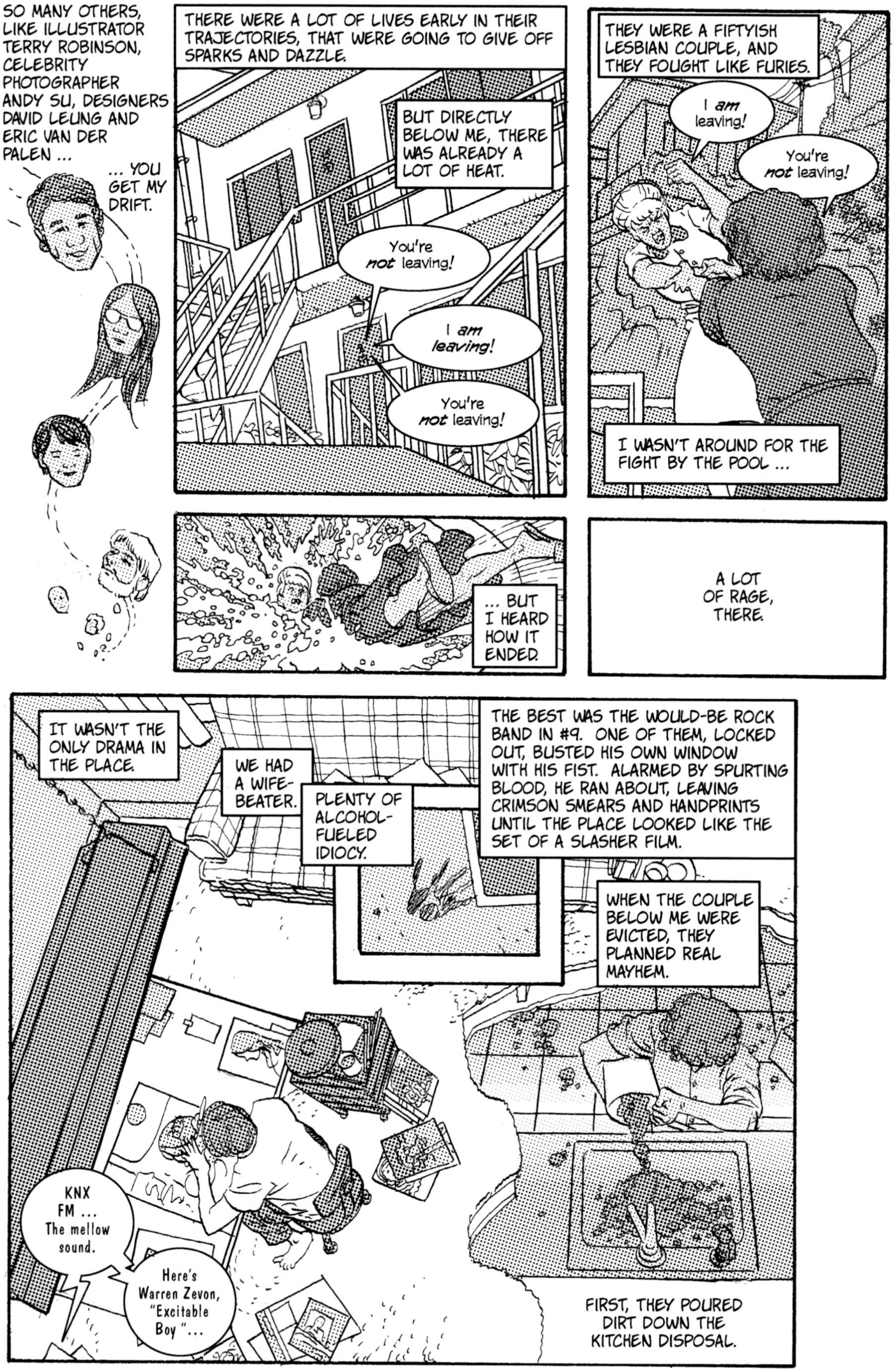

SO MANY OTHERS, LIKE ILLUSTRATOR TERRY ROBINSON, CELEBRITY PHOTOGRAPHER ANDY SU, DESIGNERS DAVID LEUNG AND ERIC VAN DER PALEN ...
... YOU GET MY DRIFT.
THERE WERE A LOT OF LIVES EARLY IN THEIR TRAJECTORIES, THAT WERE GOING TO GIVE OFF SPARKS AND DAZZLE.
BUT DIRECTLY BELOW ME, THERE WAS ALREADY A LOT OF HEAT.
You're *not* leaving!
I *am* *leaving*!
You're *not* leaving!
THEY WERE A FIFTYISH LESBIAN COUPLE, AND THEY FOUGHT LIKE FURIES.
I *am* leaving!
You're *not* leaving!
I WASN'T AROUND FOR THE FIGHT BY THE POOL ...
... BUT I HEARD HOW IT ENDED.
A LOT OF RAGE, THERE.
IT WASN'T THE ONLY DRAMA IN THE PLACE.
WE HAD A WIFE-BEATER.
PLENTY OF ALCOHOL-FUELED IDIOCY.
THE BEST WAS THE WOULD-BE ROCK BAND IN #9. ONE OF THEM, LOCKED OUT, BUSTED HIS OWN WINDOW WITH HIS FIST. ALARMED BY SPURTING BLOOD, HE RAN ABOUT, LEAVING CRIMSON SMEARS AND HANDPRINTS UNTIL THE PLACE LOOKED LIKE THE SET OF A SLASHER FILM.
WHEN THE COUPLE BELOW ME WERE EVICTED, THEY PLANNED REAL MAYHEM.
KNX FM ... The mellow sound.
Here's Warren Zevon, "Excitable Boy"...
FIRST, THEY POURED DIRT DOWN THE KITCHEN DISPOSAL.

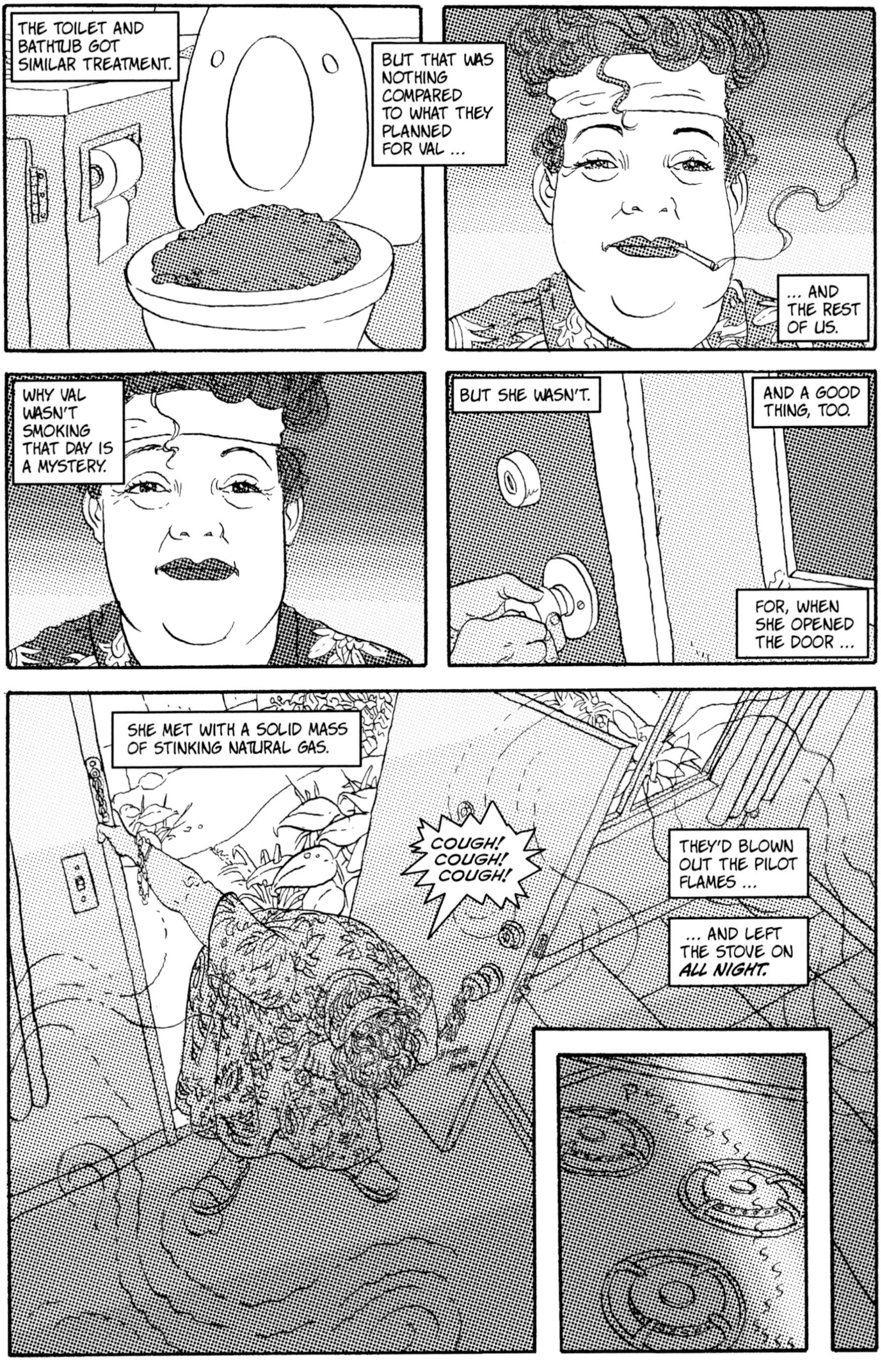
THE TOILET AND BATHTUB GOT SIMILAR TREATMENT.
BUT THAT WAS NOTHING COMPARED TO WHAT THEY PLANNED FOR VAL ...
... AND THE REST OF US.
WHY VAL WASN'T SMOKING THAT DAY IS A MYSTERY.
BUT SHE WASN'T.
AND A GOOD THING, TOO.
FOR, WHEN SHE OPENED THE DOOR ...
SHE MET WITH A SOLID MASS OF STINKING NATURAL GAS.
COUGH! COUGH! COUGH!
THEY'D BLOWN OUT THE PILOT FLAMES ...
... AND LEFT THE STOVE ON ALL NIGHT.

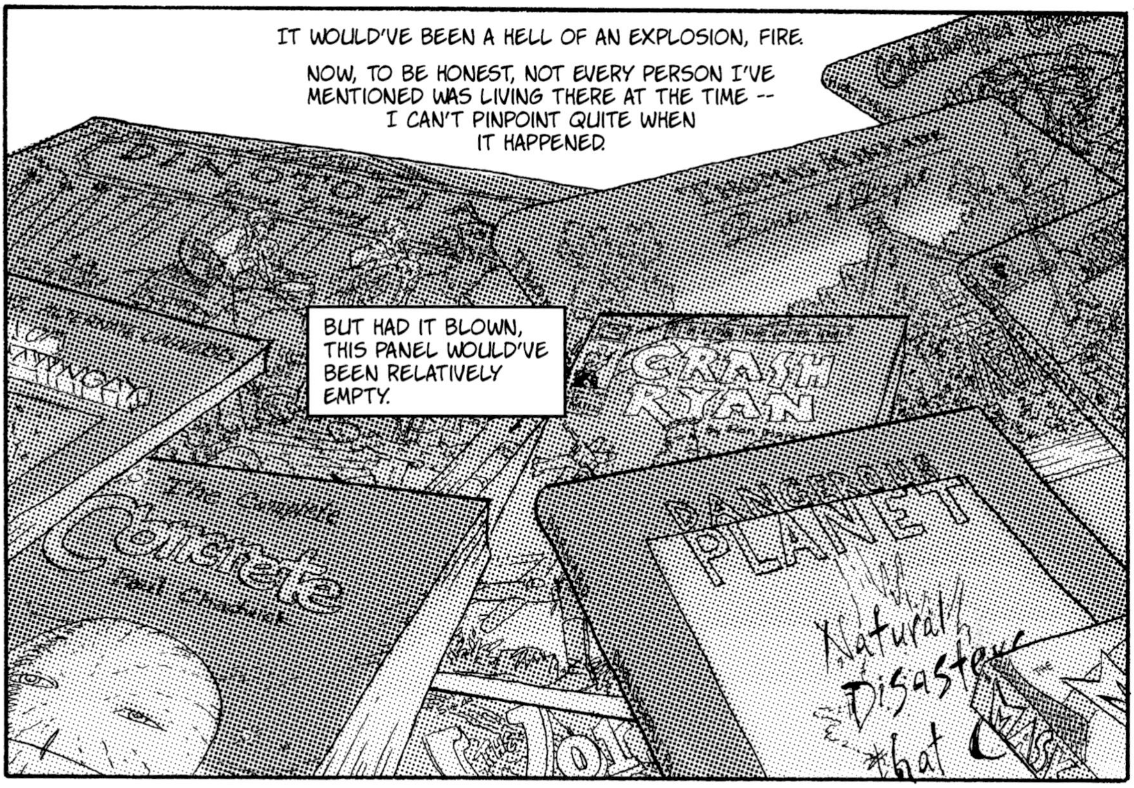
IT WOULD'VE BEEN A HELL OF AN EXPLOSION, FIRE.
NOW, TO BE HONEST, NOT EVERY PERSON I'VE MENTIONED WAS LIVING THERE AT THE TIME -- I CAN'T PINPOINT QUITE WHEN IT HAPPENED.
BUT HAD IT BLOWN, THIS PANEL WOULD'VE BEEN RELATIVELY EMPTY.
CRASH RYAN
The Complete Concrete
Paul Chadwick
PLANET
Natural Disasters that

THE VERY HUMAN QUESTION TO ASK IS: WHY WERE WE SPARED?

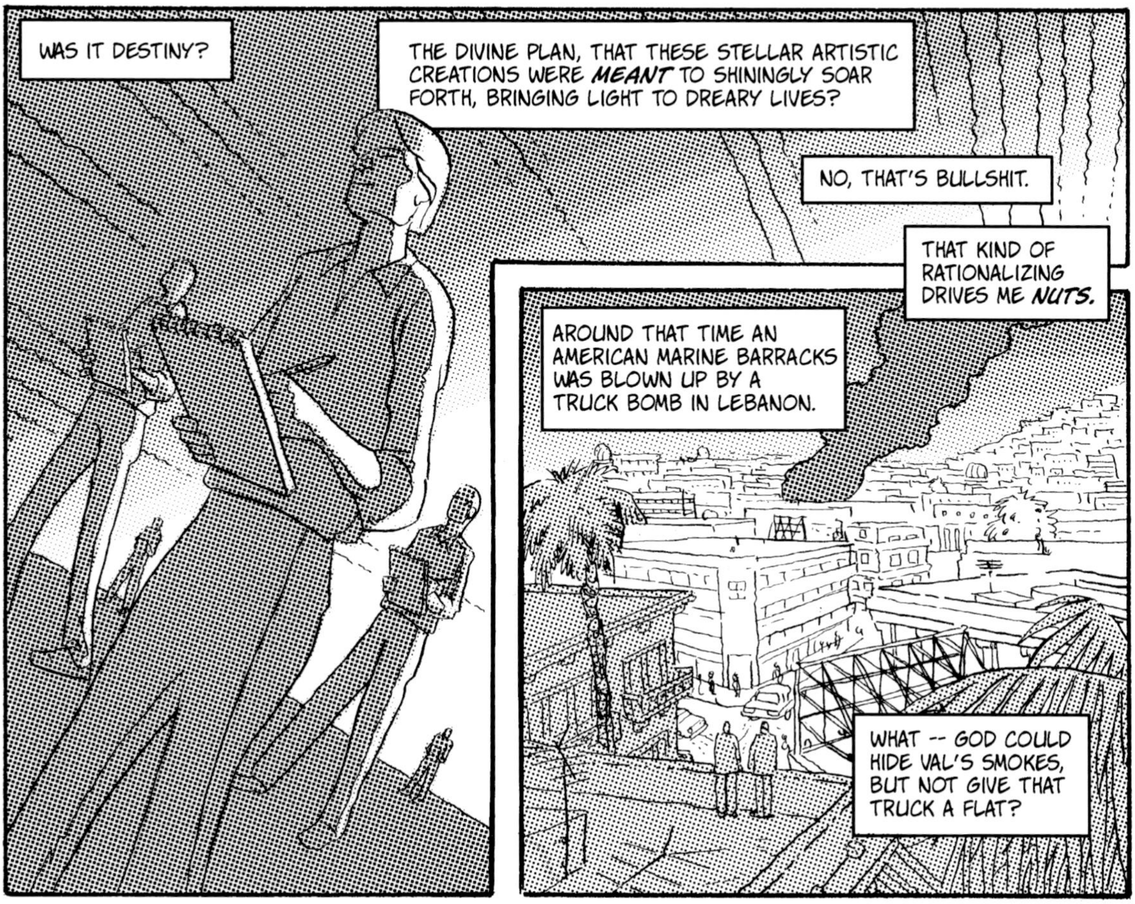
WAS IT DESTINY?
THE DIVINE PLAN, THAT THESE STELLAR ARTISTIC CREATIONS WERE *MEANT* TO SHININGLY SOAR FORTH, BRINGING LIGHT TO DREARY LIVES?
NO, THAT'S BULLSHIT.
THAT KIND OF RATIONALIZING DRIVES ME *NUTS.*
AROUND THAT TIME AN AMERICAN MARINE BARRACKS WAS BLOWN UP BY A TRUCK BOMB IN LEBANON.
WHAT -- GOD COULD HIDE VAL'S SMOKES, BUT NOT GIVE THAT TRUCK A FLAT?

YOU'RE PROBABLY FAMILIAR WITH THE "MIRACLES" THAT KEPT SO MANY FROM GETTING TO THEIR JOBS AT THE TWIN TOWERS ON SEPTEMBER 11, 2001.

ARTICLE AFTER ARTICLE, ABOUT THE COLDS, MISSED TRAINS, AND DENTIST APPOINTMENTS THAT SAVED FOLK.

AS GOD WAS SO PREOCCUPIED WITH ALL THAT, I GUESS HE FORGOT TO GIVE 19 GUYS SIMULTANEOUS HEART ATTACKS.

Allah ... akbar!

NOW, *THAT* WOULD'VE IMPRESSED ME.

FORGIVE MY SARCASM.

BUT THE FLIP SIDE OF "SAVED FOR A PURPOSE" IS "DIED FOR A PURPOSE."

WHICH IS INCHES AWAY FROM "THOSE SIX MILLION JEWS DESERVED IT."

OR "*AIDS* IS GOD'S JUDGMENT ON HOMOSEXUALS."

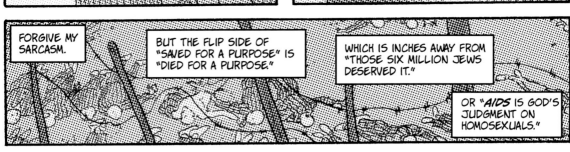

SO WHENEVER I HEAR, "IT'S ALL PART OF A PLAN" OR "ALL FOR THE BEST" FROM A CHRISTIAN OR NEW-AGER, MY TEETH GRIND.

THIS SENTIMENT IS ALWAYS EXPRESSED BY THE LUCKY WINNERS IN LIFE, UNTOUCHED BY HISTORY'S HEAVY TREAD.

IT IS NOT SHARED BY ALL RELIGIOUS THINKERS, THANKFULLY.

C.S. LEWIS GRAPPLED WITH GOD'S TOLERANCE OF EVIL IN THE *PROBLEM OF PAIN*.

HIS BELIEF: IF THE UNIVERSE WASN'T INERT, UNINTERFERED WITH BY THE DIVINE, MAN'S FREE WILL WOULD BE COMPROMISED.

GOD MADE MAN FOR FELLOWSHIP. FOR THAT, HE MUST BE FREE.

YOU CAN'T HAVE FELLOWSHIP WITH YOUR SLAVE.

AFTER LOSING A SON TO A HORRIFIC DISEASE, RABBI HAROLD KUSHNER WROTE *WHEN BAD THINGS HAPPEN TO GOOD PEOPLE*.

HE FEELS GOD SIMPLY DOESN'T INTERVENE -- EXCEPT TO GIVE US STRENGTH TO COPE.

LIKE THE SAYING: "GOD GIVES GREAT BURDENS; BUT HE ALSO GIVES SHOULDERS."

NOT EXACTLY, THOUGH. RABBI KUSHNER FEELS THE ORDERLINESS OF A UNIVERSE BLINDLY RUNNING ON NATURAL LAW IS A SUFFICIENT GOODNESS TO LET EVIL AND INJUSTICE EXIST IN IT.

GOD *CAN'T* MICROMANAGE, HE FEELS.

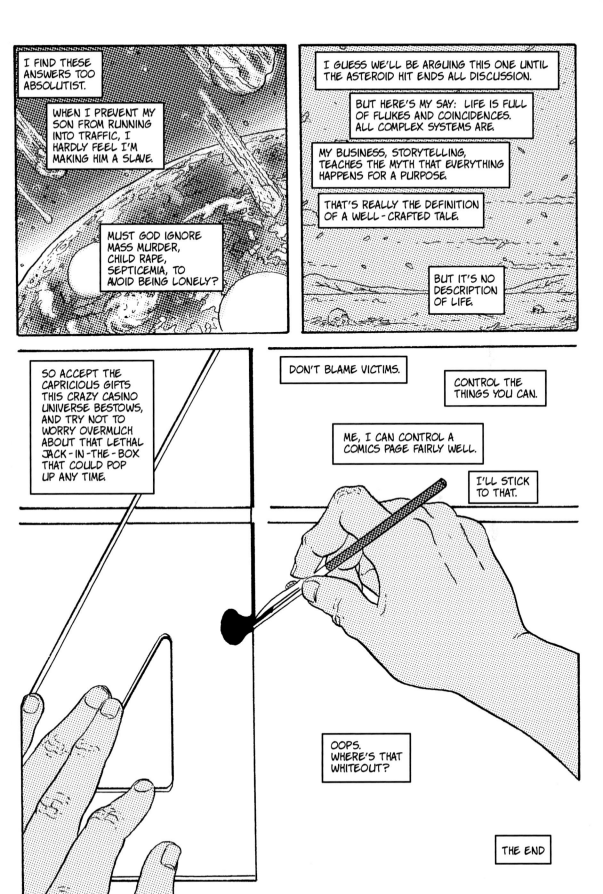

I FIND THESE ANSWERS TOO ABSOLUTIST.

WHEN I PREVENT MY SON FROM RUNNING INTO TRAFFIC, I HARDLY FEEL I'M MAKING HIM A SLAVE.

MUST GOD IGNORE MASS MURDER, CHILD RAPE, SEPTICEMIA, TO AVOID BEING LONELY?

I GUESS WE'LL BE ARGUING THIS ONE UNTIL THE ASTEROID HIT ENDS ALL DISCUSSION.

BUT HERE'S MY SAY: LIFE IS FULL OF FLUKES AND COINCIDENCES. ALL COMPLEX SYSTEMS ARE.

MY BUSINESS, STORYTELLING, TEACHES THE MYTH THAT EVERYTHING HAPPENS FOR A PURPOSE.

THAT'S REALLY THE DEFINITION OF A WELL-CRAFTED TALE.

BUT IT'S NO DESCRIPTION OF LIFE.

SO ACCEPT THE CAPRICIOUS GIFTS THIS CRAZY CASINO UNIVERSE BESTOWS, AND TRY NOT TO WORRY OVERMUCH ABOUT THAT LETHAL JACK-IN-THE-BOX THAT COULD POP UP ANY TIME.

DON'T BLAME VICTIMS.

CONTROL THE THINGS YOU CAN.

ME, I CAN CONTROL A COMICS PAGE FAIRLY WELL.

I'LL STICK TO THAT.

OOPS. WHERE'S THAT WHITEOUT?

THE END

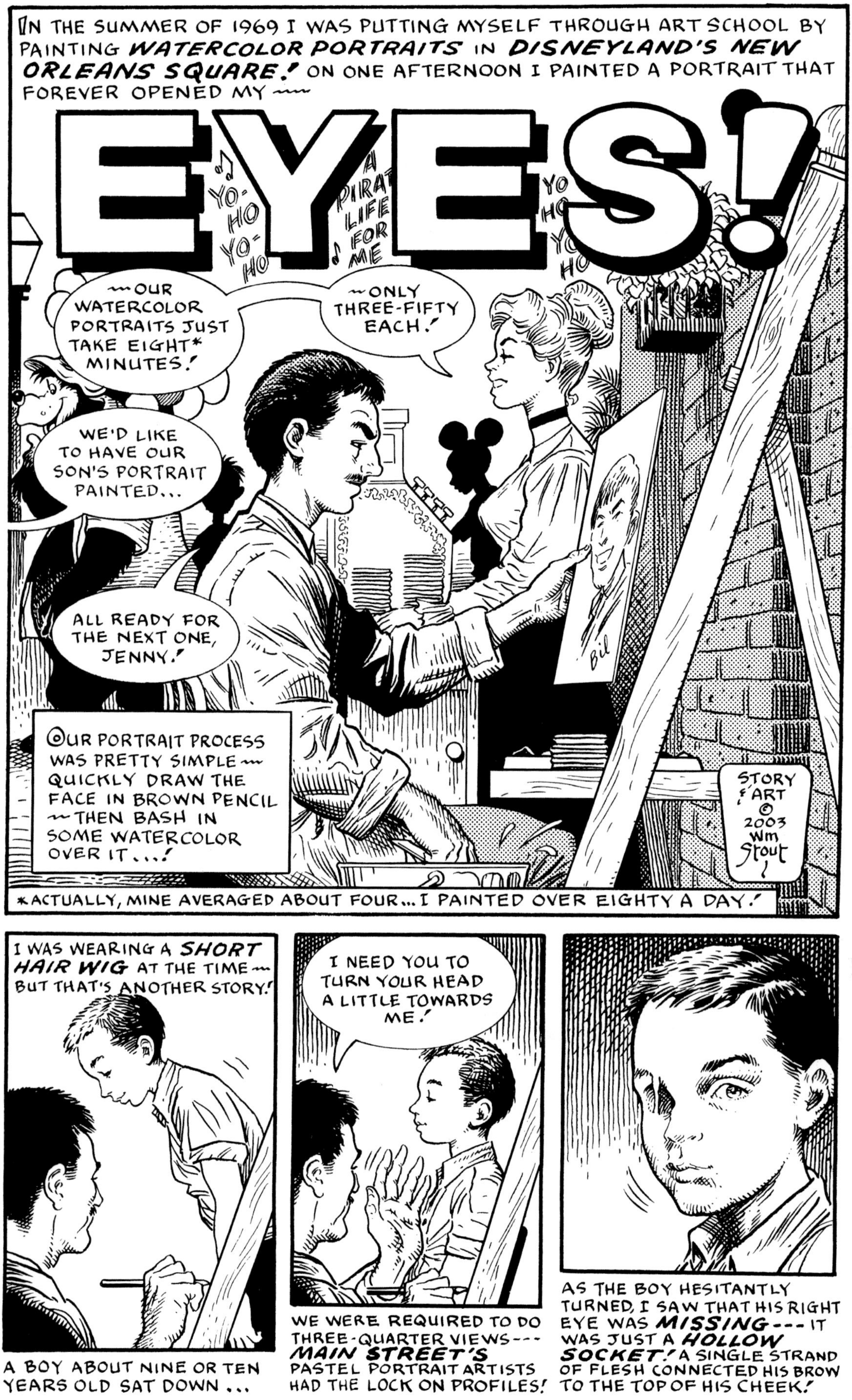
IN THE SUMMER OF 1969 I WAS PUTTING MYSELF THROUGH ART SCHOOL BY PAINTING WATERCOLOR PORTRAITS IN DISNEYLAND'S NEW ORLEANS SQUARE! ON ONE AFTERNOON I PAINTED A PORTRAIT THAT FOREVER OPENED MY ~~
EYES!
YO-HO YO-HO
A PIRATE LIFE FOR ME
YO HO YO HO
~~OUR WATERCOLOR PORTRAITS JUST TAKE EIGHT* MINUTES!
~ONLY THREE-FIFTY EACH!
WE'D LIKE TO HAVE OUR SON'S PORTRAIT PAINTED...
ALL READY FOR THE NEXT ONE, JENNY!
Bil
OUR PORTRAIT PROCESS WAS PRETTY SIMPLE ~~ QUICKLY DRAW THE FACE IN BROWN PENCIL ~~ THEN BASH IN SOME WATERCOLOR OVER IT...!
STORY & ART © 2003 Wm Stout
*ACTUALLY, MINE AVERAGED ABOUT FOUR... I PAINTED OVER EIGHTY A DAY!
I WAS WEARING A SHORT HAIR WIG AT THE TIME ~~ BUT THAT'S ANOTHER STORY!
A BOY ABOUT NINE OR TEN YEARS OLD SAT DOWN...
I NEED YOU TO TURN YOUR HEAD A LITTLE TOWARDS ME!
WE WERE REQUIRED TO DO THREE-QUARTER VIEWS--- MAIN STREET'S PASTEL PORTRAIT ARTISTS HAD THE LOCK ON PROFILES!
AS THE BOY HESITANTLY TURNED, I SAW THAT HIS RIGHT EYE WAS MISSING--- IT WAS JUST A HOLLOW SOCKET! A SINGLE STRAND OF FLESH CONNECTED HIS BROW TO THE TOP OF HIS CHEEK!

JEEZ! WHAT IN THE HECK AM I GONNA *DO?*

DO HIS PARENTS EXPECT ME TO DRAW HIM *AS IS* ---? OR SHOULD I DRAW HIM WITH TWO "GOOD" EYES?

I COULD FEEL THE PRESENCE AND TENSION OF THE PARENTS BEHIND ME AS MY PENCIL APPROACHED THE BOARD!

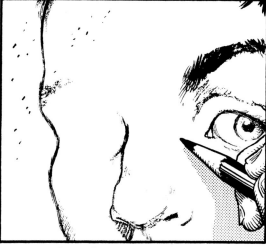

I DREW HIS LEFT EYE AND THEN THE REST OF HIS FACE! I SLOWLY SKETCHED, STALLING FOR TIME AS I TRIED TO GET A "READ" ON HIS PARENTS...

BY NOW THE TENSION WAS ALMOST *PALPABLE!* I COULDN'T DELAY ANY LONGER! I FINALLY WENT WITH MY GUT AND MADE A DECISION...

I TOOK A DEEP BREATH...
...AND I BEGAN TO DRAW...

I CHOSE TO DRAW THEIR YOUNG SON WITH *TWO PERFECT EYES!*

FROM BEHIND ME I HEARD TWO HUGE, AUDIBLE SIGHS OF *RELIEF!*

AS I FILLED THE SKETCH IN WITH PAINT, I KNEW I HAD MADE THE RIGHT DECISION!

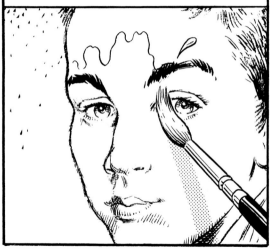

IN HIS PARENTS' EYES, THEIR SON WAS NOT DEFORMED AT ALL; HE WAS THEIR *PERFECT LITTLE BOY!*

HERE YOU ARE!

IT WAS JENNY THE CASHIER'S JOB TO PRESENT THE FINISHED PORTRAITS...

I WATCHED THEM WALK AWAY...

END

I FELT SO GRATEFUL THAT MY PAINTING OF THEIR SON BROUGHT THEM SO MUCH JOY, AND THAT I, ALSO, HAD BEEN BLESSED BY LUCK AND INSTINCT TO PORTRAY THAT SWEET BOY THROUGH THEIR EYES ~~~ THE *EYES* OF *LOVE!!*

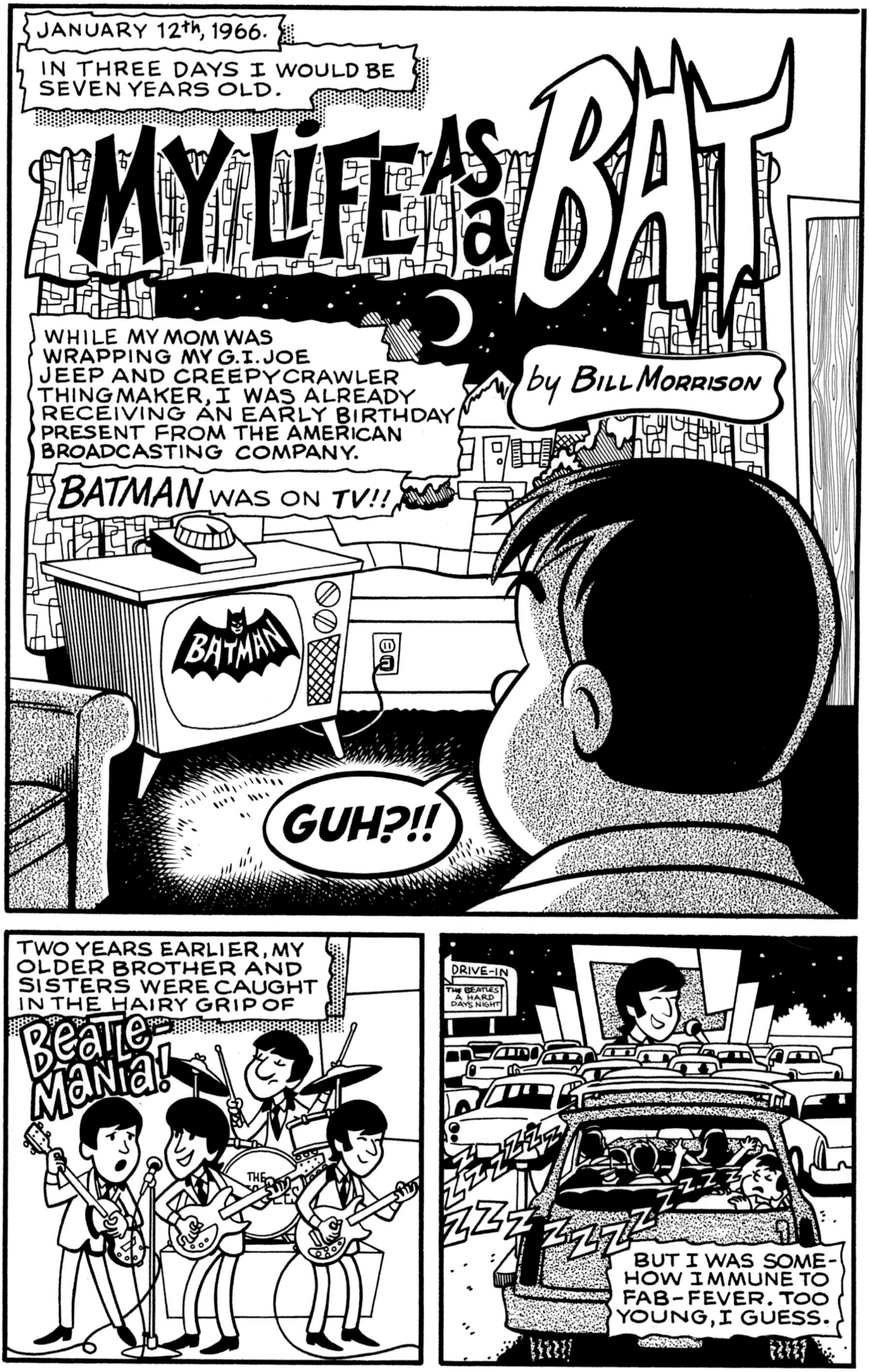
JANUARY 12th, 1966.
IN THREE DAYS I WOULD BE SEVEN YEARS OLD.
MY LIFE AS a BAT
by BILL MORRISON
WHILE MY MOM WAS WRAPPING MY G.I. JOE JEEP AND CREEPY CRAWLER THINGMAKER, I WAS ALREADY RECEIVING AN EARLY BIRTHDAY PRESENT FROM THE AMERICAN BROADCASTING COMPANY.
BATMAN WAS ON TV!!
BATMAN
GUH?!!
TWO YEARS EARLIER, MY OLDER BROTHER AND SISTERS WERE CAUGHT IN THE HAIRY GRIP OF
Beatle-Mania!
DRIVE-IN
THE BEATLES A HARD DAYS NIGHT
ZZZZZ
ZZZ
ZZZZZZ
BUT I WAS SOME-HOW IMMUNE TO FAB-FEVER. TOO YOUNG, I GUESS.

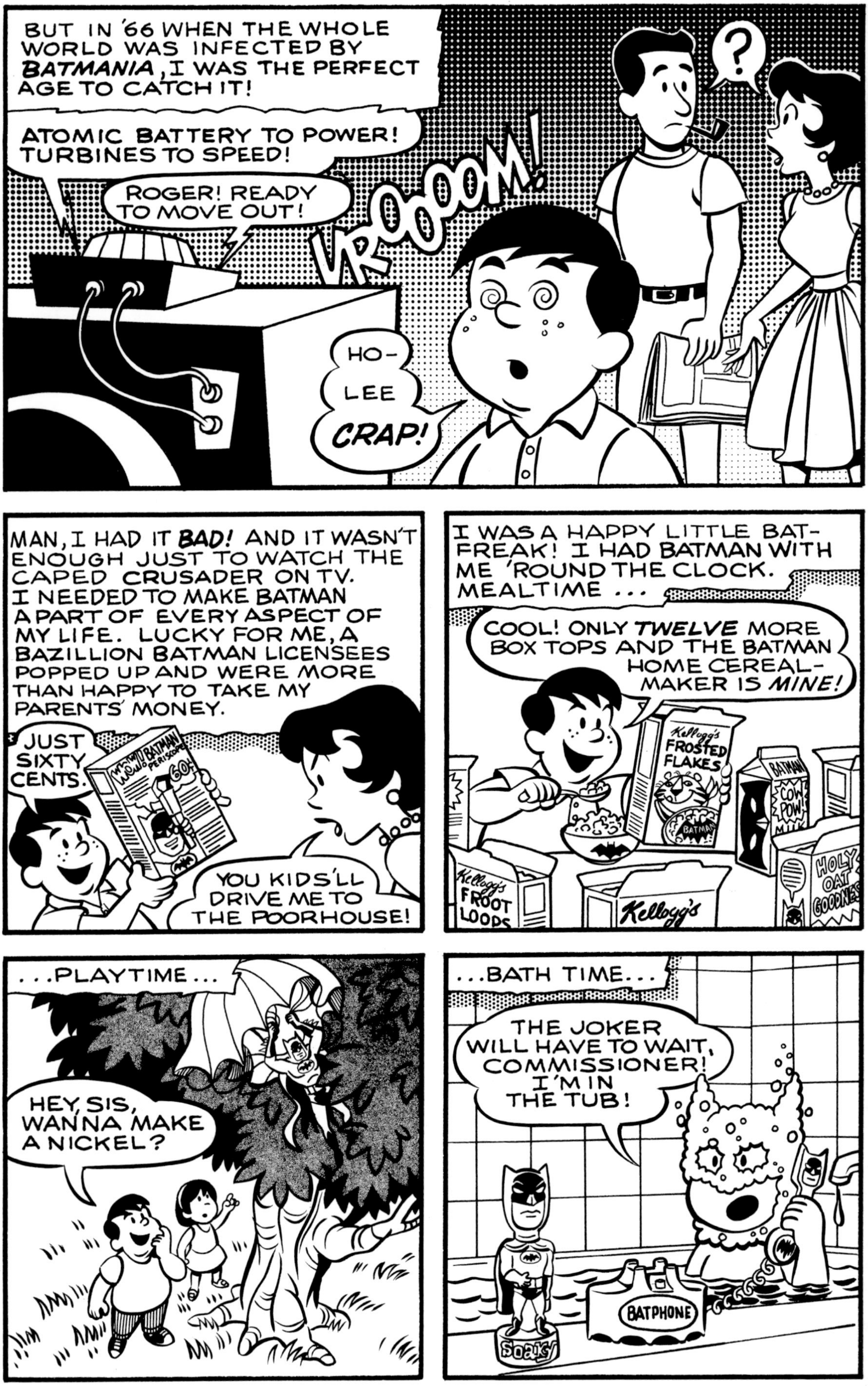

BUT IN '66 WHEN THE WHOLE WORLD WAS INFECTED BY BATMANIA, I WAS THE PERFECT AGE TO CATCH IT!
ATOMIC BATTERY TO POWER! TURBINES TO SPEED!
ROGER! READY TO MOVE OUT!
VROOOOM!
?
HO- LEE CRAP!
MAN, I HAD IT BAD! AND IT WASN'T ENOUGH JUST TO WATCH THE CAPED CRUSADER ON TV. I NEEDED TO MAKE BATMAN A PART OF EVERY ASPECT OF MY LIFE. LUCKY FOR ME, A BAZILLION BATMAN LICENSEES POPPED UP AND WERE MORE THAN HAPPY TO TAKE MY PARENTS' MONEY.
JUST SIXTY CENTS.
BATMAN PERISCOPE
60¢
YOU KIDS'LL DRIVE ME TO THE POORHOUSE!
I WAS A HAPPY LITTLE BAT-FREAK! I HAD BATMAN WITH ME 'ROUND THE CLOCK. MEALTIME ...
COOL! ONLY TWELVE MORE BOX TOPS AND THE BATMAN HOME CEREAL-MAKER IS MINE!
Kellogg's FROSTED FLAKES
BATMAN
COW POW!
Kellogg's FROOT LOOPS
Kellogg's
HOLY OAT GOODNES
...PLAYTIME...
HEY, SIS, WANNA MAKE A NICKEL?
...BATH TIME...
THE JOKER WILL HAVE TO WAIT, COMMISSIONER! I'M IN THE TUB!
BATPHONE
Soaky

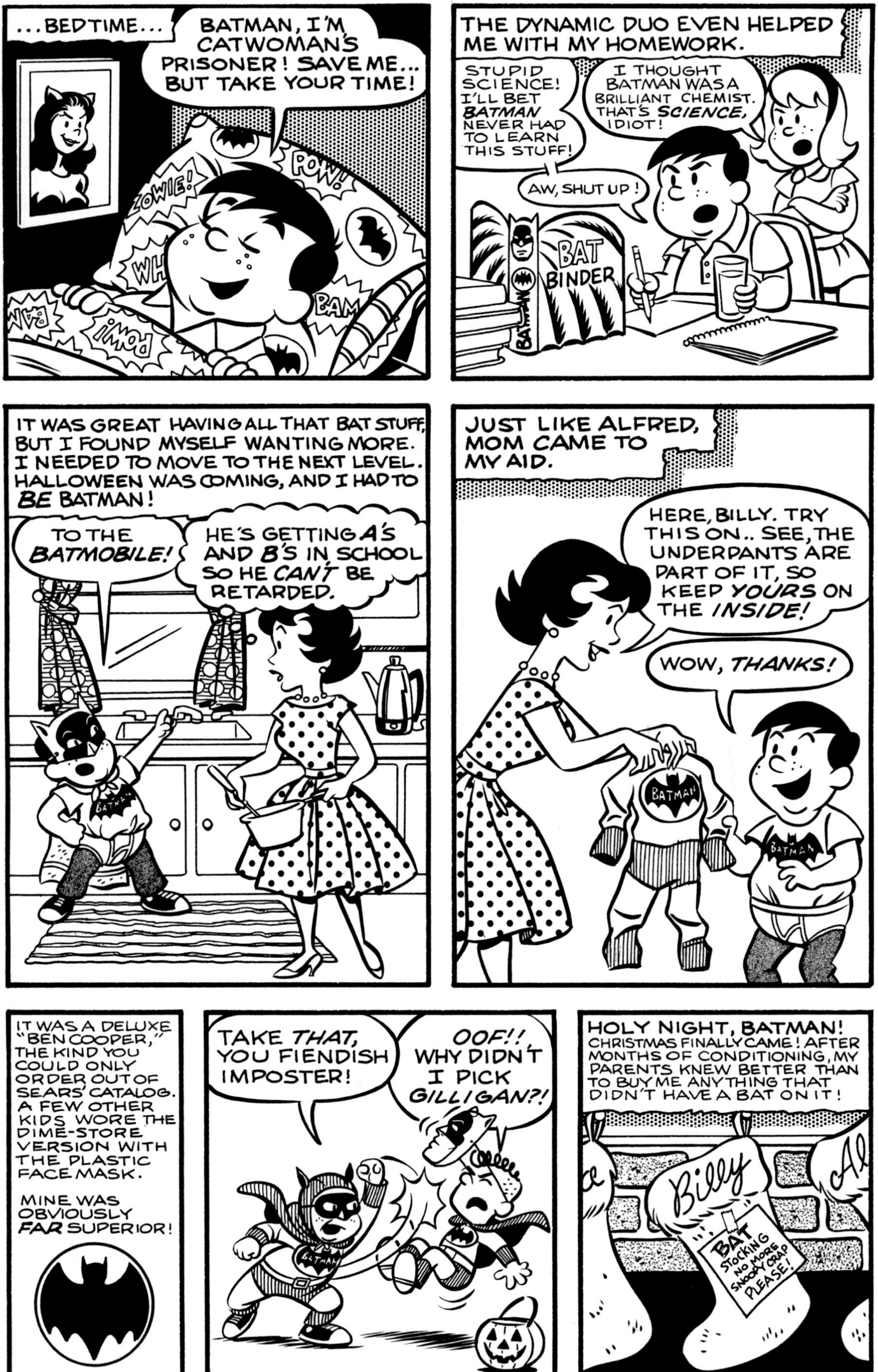
...BEDTIME...
BATMAN, I'M CATWOMAN'S PRISONER! SAVE ME... BUT TAKE YOUR TIME!
ZOWIE!
POW!
WH
BAM
BAM
POW!
THE DYNAMIC DUO EVEN HELPED ME WITH MY HOMEWORK.
STUPID SCIENCE! I'LL BET BATMAN NEVER HAD TO LEARN THIS STUFF!
I THOUGHT BATMAN WAS A BRILLIANT CHEMIST. THAT'S SCIENCE, IDIOT!
AW, SHUT UP!
BAT BINDER
BATMAN
IT WAS GREAT HAVING ALL THAT BAT STUFF, BUT I FOUND MYSELF WANTING MORE. I NEEDED TO MOVE TO THE NEXT LEVEL. HALLOWEEN WAS COMING, AND I HAD TO BE BATMAN!
TO THE BATMOBILE!
HE'S GETTING A'S AND B'S IN SCHOOL SO HE CAN'T BE RETARDED.
BATMAN
JUST LIKE ALFRED, MOM CAME TO MY AID.
HERE, BILLY. TRY THIS ON.. SEE, THE UNDERPANTS ARE PART OF IT, SO KEEP YOURS ON THE INSIDE!
WOW, THANKS!
BATMAN
BATMAN
IT WAS A DELUXE "BEN COOPER," THE KIND YOU COULD ONLY ORDER OUT OF SEARS' CATALOG. A FEW OTHER KIDS WORE THE DIME-STORE VERSION WITH THE PLASTIC FACE MASK.
MINE WAS OBVIOUSLY FAR SUPERIOR!
TAKE THAT, YOU FIENDISH IMPOSTER!
OOF!! WHY DIDN'T I PICK GILLIGAN?!
BATMAN
HOLY NIGHT, BATMAN! CHRISTMAS FINALLY CAME! AFTER MONTHS OF CONDITIONING, MY PARENTS KNEW BETTER THAN TO BUY ME ANYTHING THAT DIDN'T HAVE A BAT ON IT!
Billy
BAT STOCKING NO MORE SNOOPY CRAP PLEASE!

I GOT A LOT OF GOOD STUFF THAT YEAR, BUT BEST OF ALL WAS A GIFT FROM MY AUNT AND UNCLE: A SUPER-DELUXE UP-GRADE TO MY ALREADY GREAT COSTUME!

BIG, GOOFY PLASTIC HELMET

CHUBBY FACE CONCEALED BY HELMET

RUSTY, IN OLD MASK & CAPE

GADGET-LADEN UTILITY BELT

BATWING-SCALLOPED PLASTIC CAPE

BATMAN

THIS WAS NOW A COSTUME FOR *PLAYING* IN, NOT JUST TRICK-OR-TREATING. BUT EVEN *I* FELT STUPID WEARING IT ALONE. SO I TALKED MY FRIEND JOHNNY POTTS INTO BEING THE JOKER.

THIS WAS THE BEST HE COULD COME UP WITH, BUT SOMEHOW IT WORKED AND I PRETENDED TO BEAT THE HELL OUT OF HIM AT EVERY OPPORTUNITY.

LAST CHANCE, JOKER! TELL ME WHERE YOUR MOM IS HIDING THE OREOS!

AAACK!

BUT ALL GOOD THINGS COME TO AN END, RIGHT?

BREAK IT UP, YOU LITTLE HOMOS!

HEY, IF YOU WANNA SEE A REALLY *GOOD* BATMAN COSTUME, TAKE A LOOK OUT-SIDE!

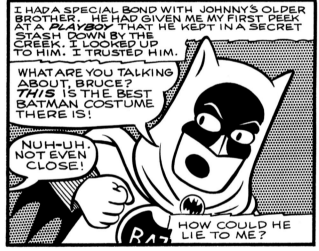

I HAD A SPECIAL BOND WITH JOHNNY'S OLDER BROTHER. HE HAD GIVEN ME MY FIRST PEEK AT A *PLAYBOY* THAT HE KEPT IN A SECRET STASH DOWN BY THE CREEK. I LOOKED UP TO HIM. I TRUSTED HIM.

WHAT ARE YOU TALKING ABOUT, BRUCE? *THIS* IS THE BEST BATMAN COSTUME THERE IS!

NUH-UH. NOT EVEN CLOSE!

HOW COULD HE LIE TO ME?

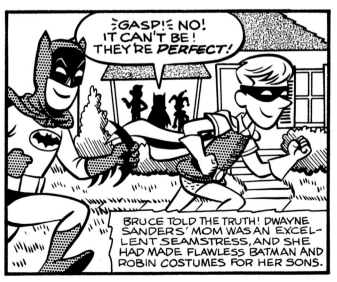

≳GASP!≲ NO! IT CAN'T BE! THEY'RE *PERFECT!*

BRUCE TOLD THE TRUTH! DWAYNE SANDERS' MOM WAS AN EXCELLENT SEAMSTRESS, AND SHE HAD MADE FLAWLESS BATMAN AND ROBIN COSTUMES FOR HER SONS.

I WAS HOPELESSLY OUTCLASSED! THERE WAS NO WAY I COULD SHOW MY HELMETED HEAD IN THE NEIGHBORHOOD AS LONG AS THE SANDERS BROTHERS WERE AROUND.

TIME TO HANG UP MY CAPE AND COWL ≳SNIFF!≲...*FOREVER!*

BATMAN

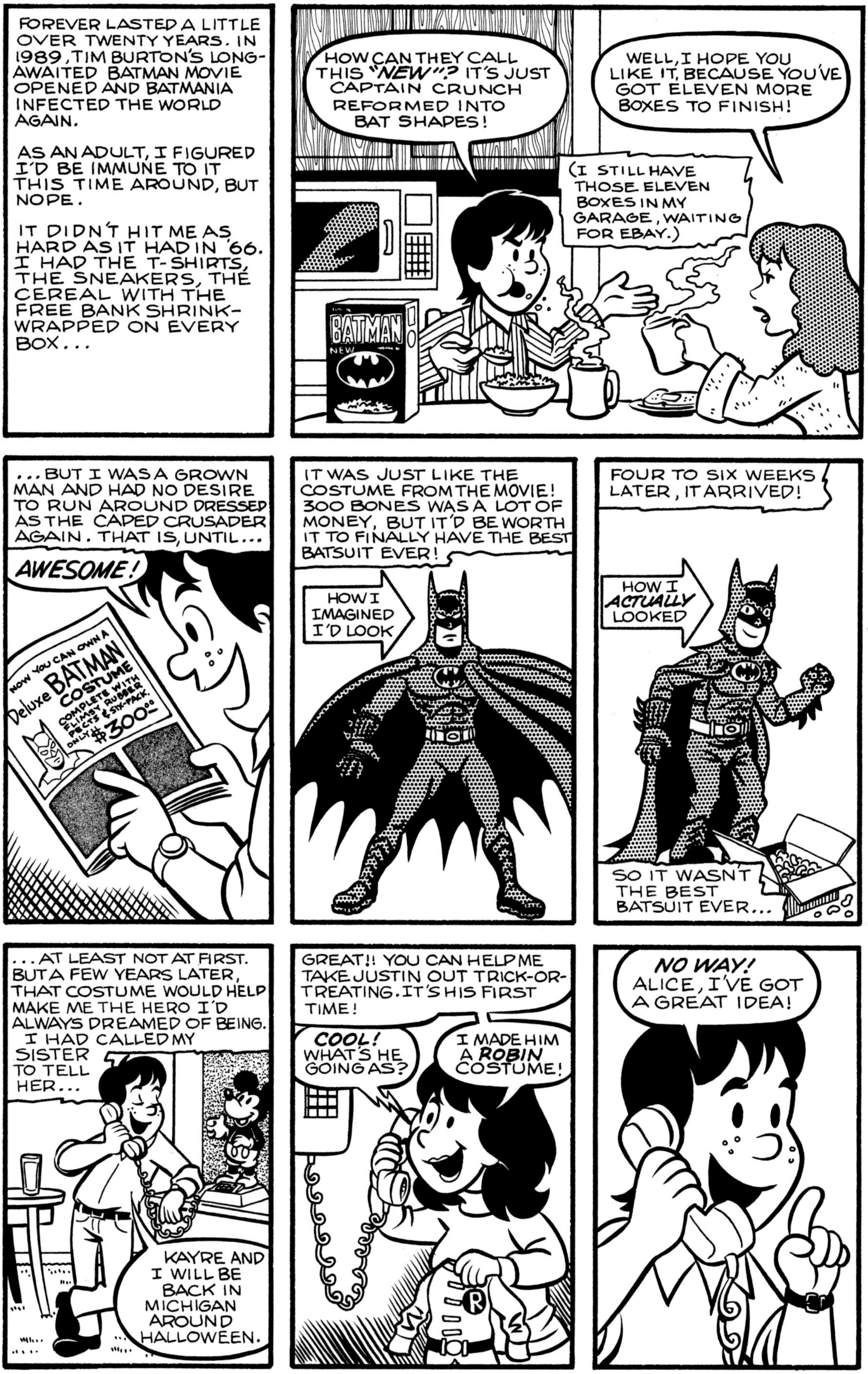
FOREVER LASTED A LITTLE OVER TWENTY YEARS. IN 1989, TIM BURTON'S LONG-AWAITED BATMAN MOVIE OPENED AND BATMANIA INFECTED THE WORLD AGAIN.
AS AN ADULT, I FIGURED I'D BE IMMUNE TO IT THIS TIME AROUND, BUT NOPE.
IT DIDN'T HIT ME AS HARD AS IT HAD IN '66. I HAD THE T-SHIRTS, THE SNEAKERS, THE CEREAL WITH THE FREE BANK SHRINK-WRAPPED ON EVERY BOX...
HOW CAN THEY CALL THIS "NEW"? IT'S JUST CAPTAIN CRUNCH REFORMED INTO BAT SHAPES!
WELL, I HOPE YOU LIKE IT, BECAUSE YOU'VE GOT ELEVEN MORE BOXES TO FINISH!
(I STILL HAVE THOSE ELEVEN BOXES IN MY GARAGE, WAITING FOR EBAY.)
BATMAN
NEW
...BUT I WAS A GROWN MAN AND HAD NO DESIRE TO RUN AROUND DRESSED AS THE CAPED CRUSADER AGAIN. THAT IS, UNTIL...
AWESOME!
NOW YOU CAN OWN A Deluxe BATMAN COSTUME COMPLETE WITH FLIMSY RUBBER PECTS & SIX-PACK. ONLY $300.00
IT WAS JUST LIKE THE COSTUME FROM THE MOVIE! 300 BONES WAS A LOT OF MONEY, BUT IT'D BE WORTH IT TO FINALLY HAVE THE BEST BATSUIT EVER!
HOW I IMAGINED I'D LOOK
FOUR TO SIX WEEKS LATER, IT ARRIVED!
HOW I ACTUALLY LOOKED
SO IT WASN'T THE BEST BATSUIT EVER...
...AT LEAST NOT AT FIRST. BUT A FEW YEARS LATER, THAT COSTUME WOULD HELP MAKE ME THE HERO I'D ALWAYS DREAMED OF BEING.
I HAD CALLED MY SISTER TO TELL HER...
KAYRE AND I WILL BE BACK IN MICHIGAN AROUND HALLOWEEN.
GREAT!! YOU CAN HELP ME TAKE JUSTIN OUT TRICK-OR-TREATING. IT'S HIS FIRST TIME!
COOL! WHAT'S HE GOING AS?
I MADE HIM A ROBIN COSTUME!
NO WAY! ALICE, I'VE GOT A GREAT IDEA!

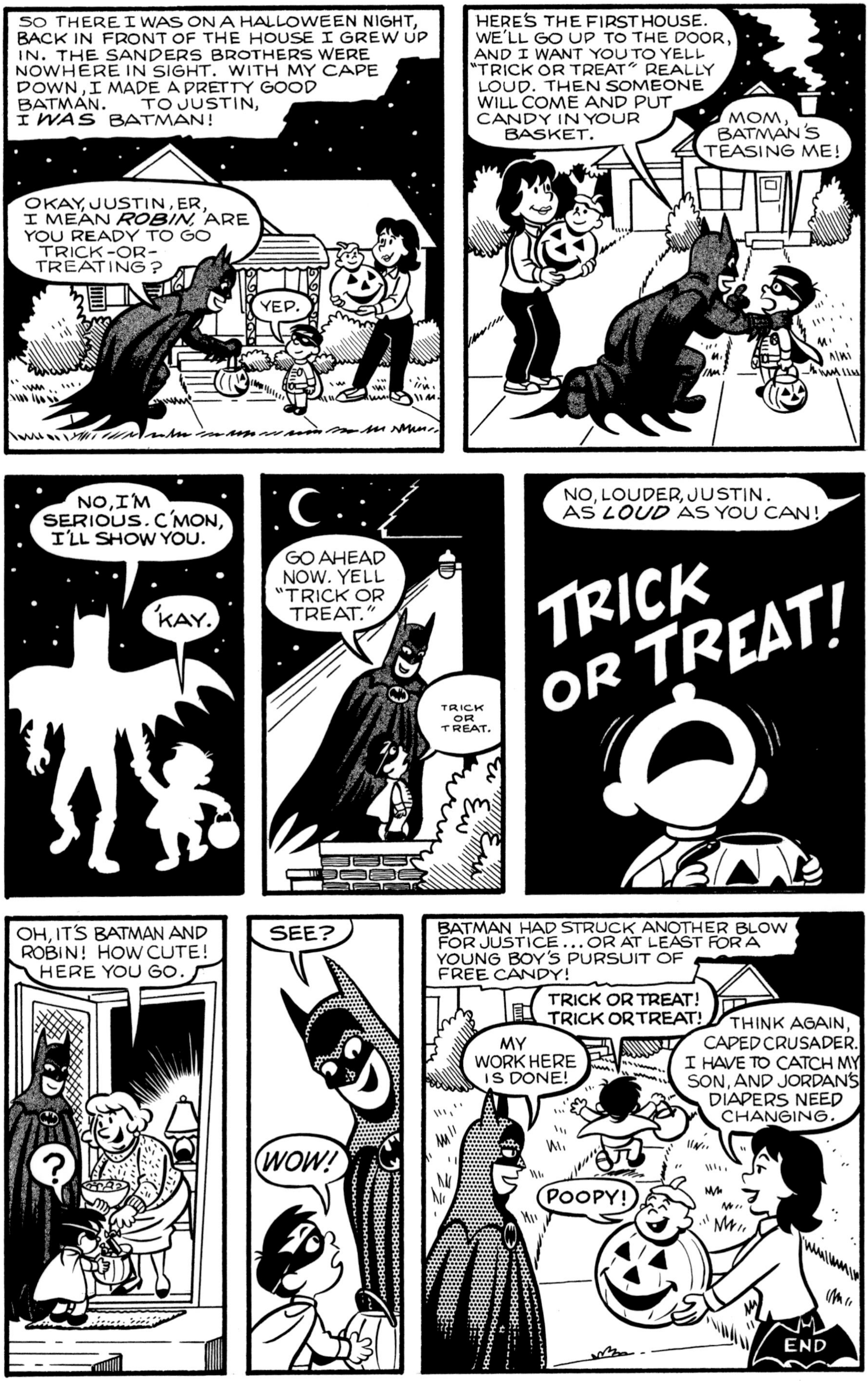
SO THERE I WAS ON A HALLOWEEN NIGHT, BACK IN FRONT OF THE HOUSE I GREW UP IN. THE SANDERS BROTHERS WERE NOWHERE IN SIGHT. WITH MY CAPE DOWN, I MADE A PRETTY GOOD BATMAN. TO JUSTIN, I WAS BATMAN!
OKAY, JUSTIN, ER, I MEAN ROBIN, ARE YOU READY TO GO TRICK-OR-TREATING?
YEP.
HERE'S THE FIRST HOUSE. WE'LL GO UP TO THE DOOR, AND I WANT YOU TO YELL "TRICK OR TREAT" REALLY LOUD. THEN SOMEONE WILL COME AND PUT CANDY IN YOUR BASKET.
MOM, BATMAN'S TEASING ME!
NO, I'M SERIOUS. C'MON, I'LL SHOW YOU.
'KAY.
GO AHEAD NOW. YELL "TRICK OR TREAT."
TRICK OR TREAT.
NO, LOUDER, JUSTIN. AS LOUD AS YOU CAN!
TRICK OR TREAT!
OH, IT'S BATMAN AND ROBIN! HOW CUTE! HERE YOU GO.
?
SEE?
WOW!
BATMAN HAD STRUCK ANOTHER BLOW FOR JUSTICE... OR AT LEAST FOR A YOUNG BOY'S PURSUIT OF FREE CANDY!
TRICK OR TREAT! TRICK OR TREAT!
MY WORK HERE IS DONE!
THINK AGAIN, CAPED CRUSADER. I HAVE TO CATCH MY SON, AND JORDAN'S DIAPERS NEED CHANGING.
POOPY!
END

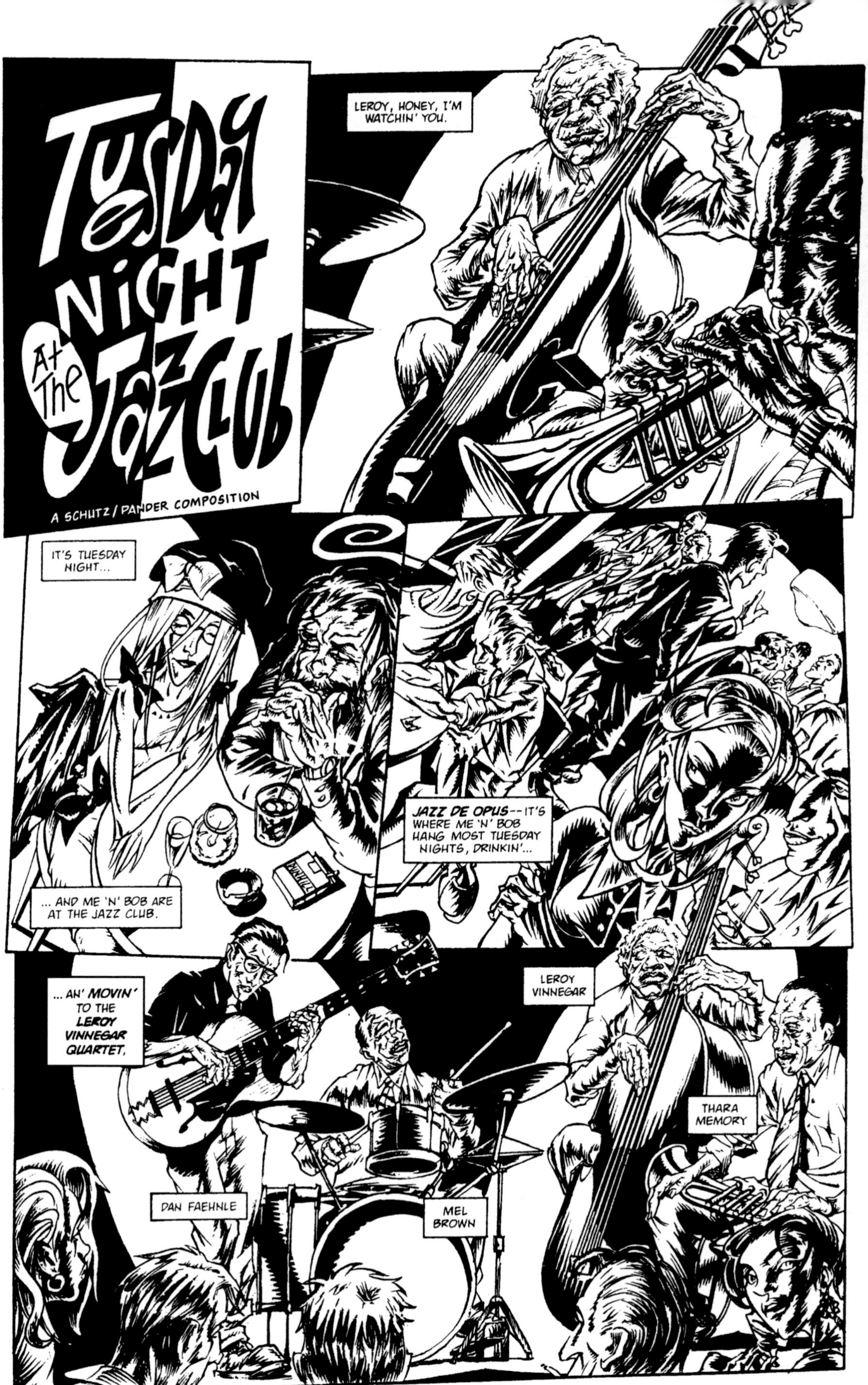
TUESDAY NIGHT At The JAZZ CLUB
A SCHUTZ/PANDER COMPOSITION
LEROY, HONEY, I'M WATCHIN' YOU.
IT'S TUESDAY NIGHT...
... AND ME 'N' BOB ARE AT THE JAZZ CLUB.
JAZZ DE OPUS--IT'S WHERE ME 'N' BOB HANG MOST TUESDAY NIGHTS, DRINKIN'...
... AN' MOVIN' TO THE LEROY VINNEGAR QUARTET,
LEROY VINNEGAR
THARA MEMORY
DAN FAEHNLE
MEL BROWN

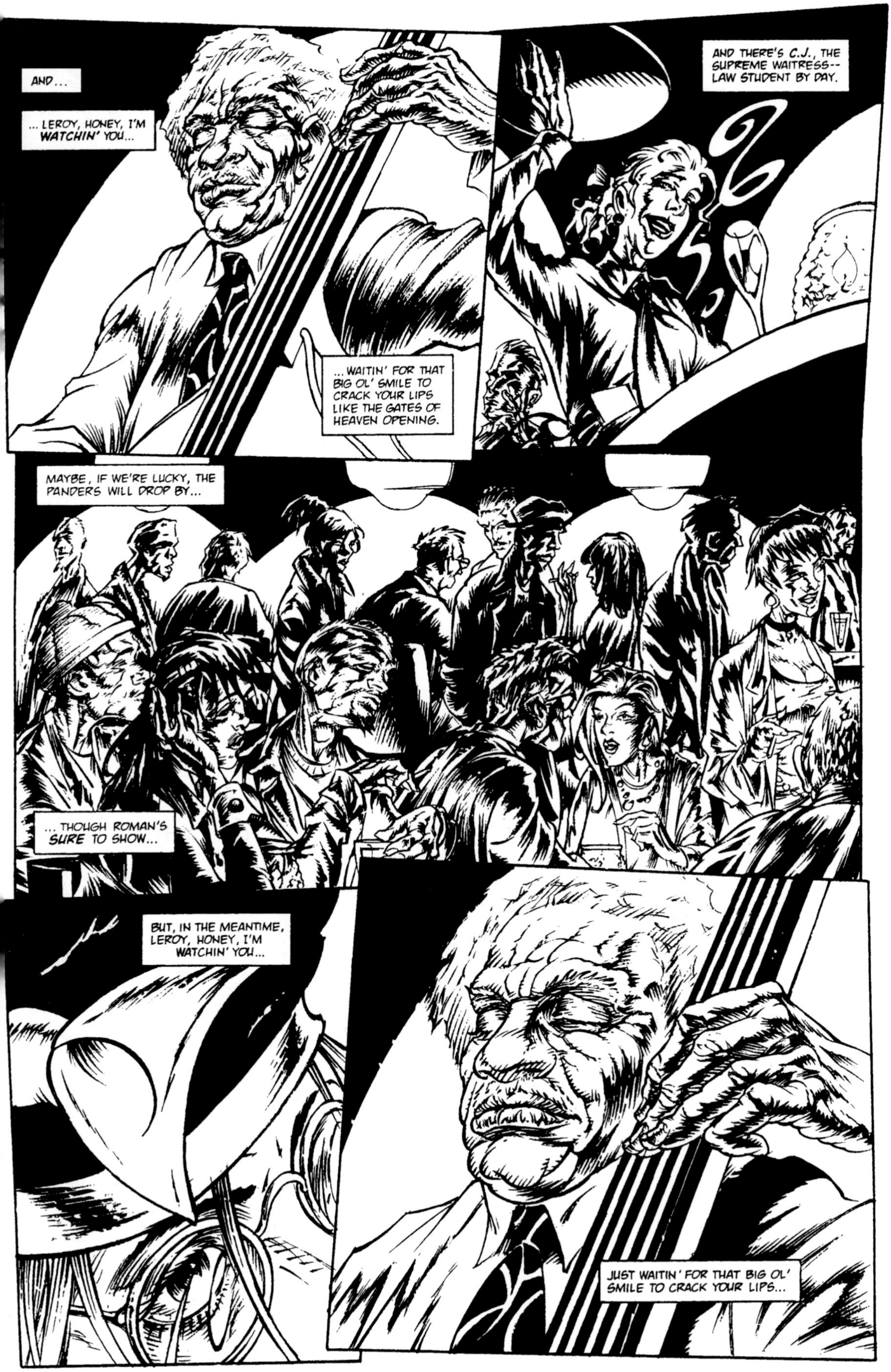
AND...
...LEROY, HONEY, I'M WATCHIN' YOU...
...WAITIN' FOR THAT BIG OL' SMILE TO CRACK YOUR LIPS LIKE THE GATES OF HEAVEN OPENING.
AND THERE'S C.J., THE SUPREME WAITRESS-- LAW STUDENT BY DAY.
MAYBE, IF WE'RE LUCKY, THE PANDERS WILL DROP BY...
...THOUGH ROMAN'S SURE TO SHOW...
BUT, IN THE MEANTIME, LEROY, HONEY, I'M WATCHIN' YOU...
JUST WAITIN' FOR THAT BIG OL' SMILE TO CRACK YOUR LIPS...

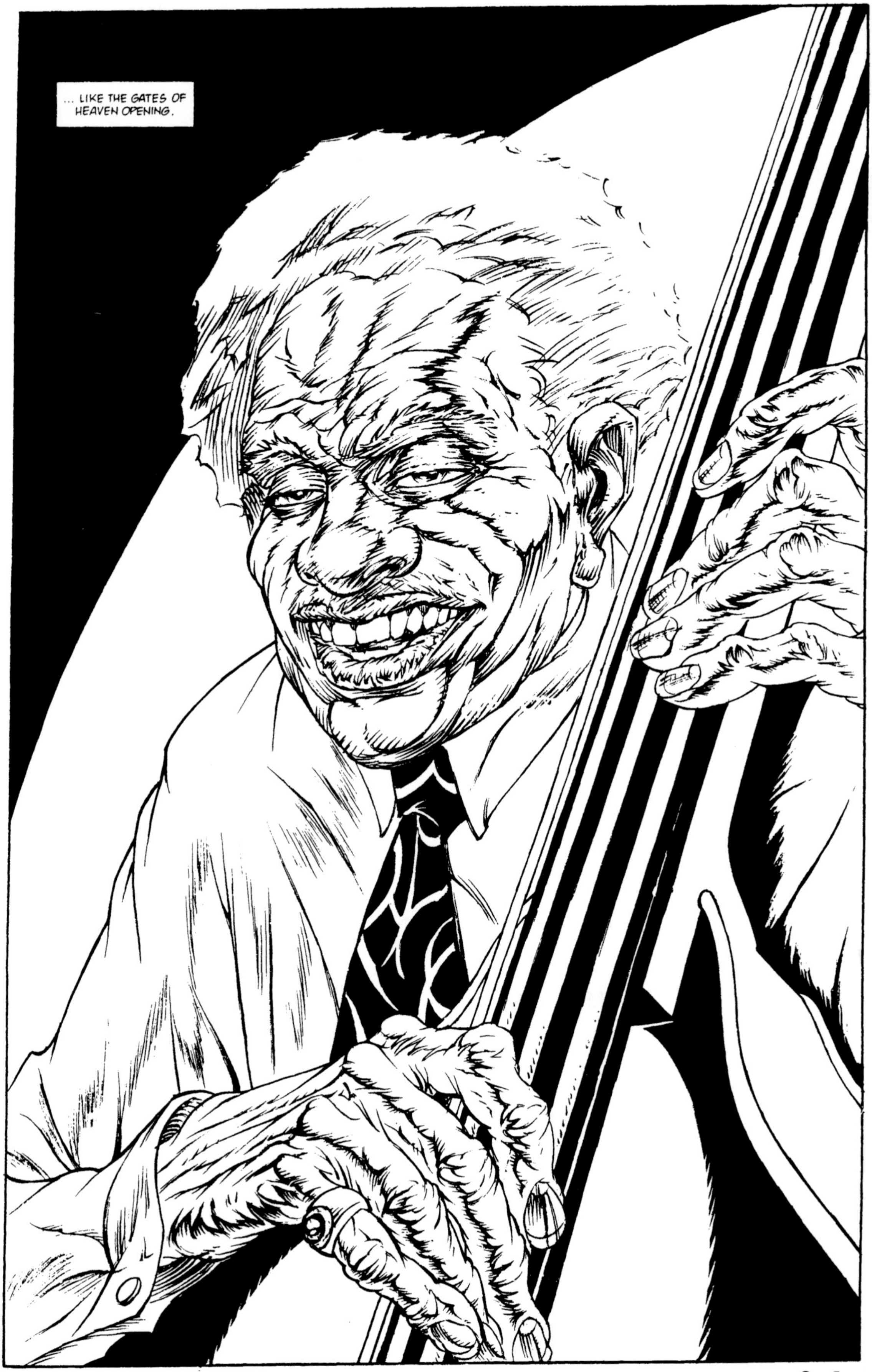
... LIKE THE GATES OF HEAVEN OPENING.

Coda

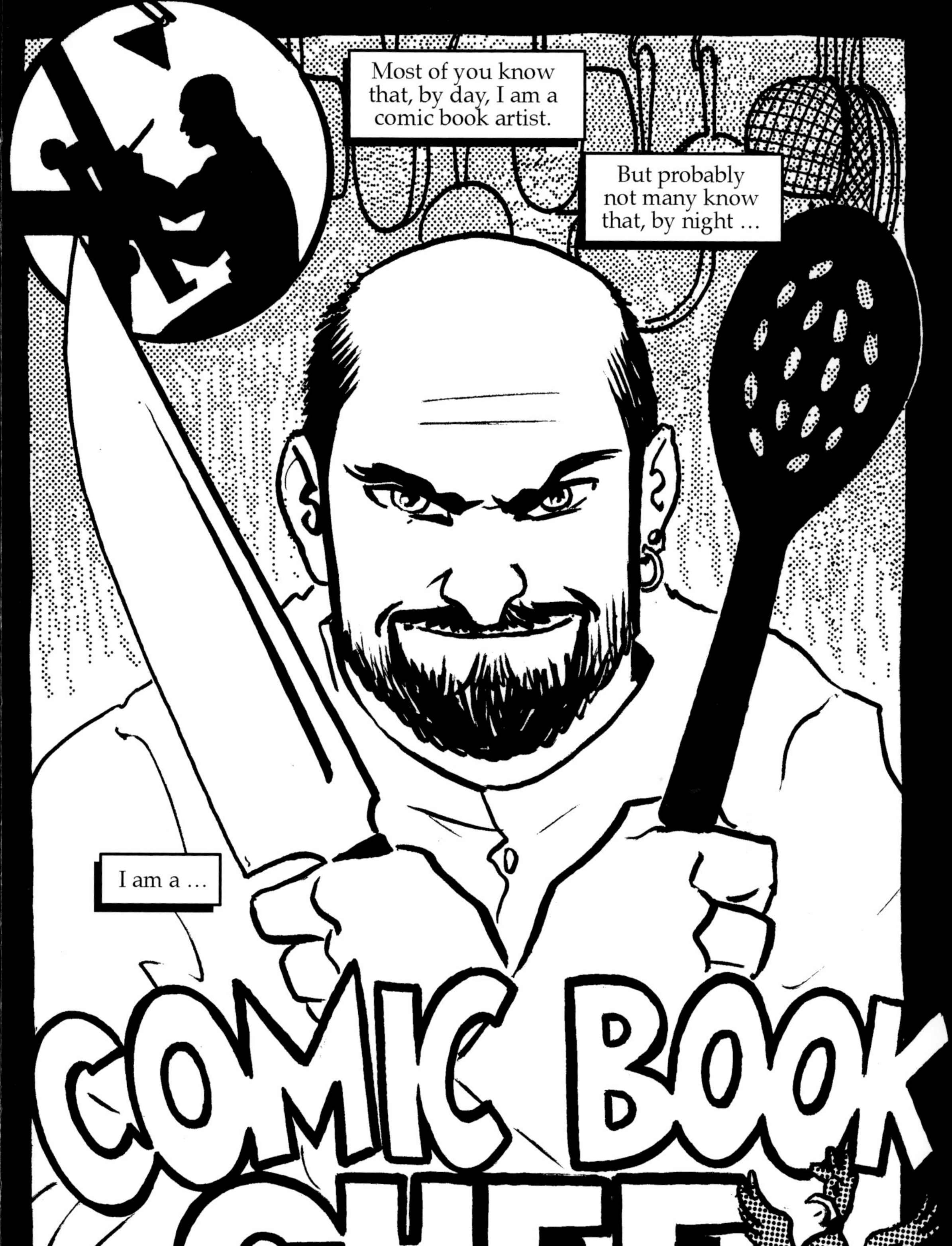
Most of you know that, by day, I am a comic book artist.
But probably not many know that, by night …
I am a …
COMIC BOOK
CHEF

And today I'm going to show you how to make an easy, and always popular, dish:

CHICKEN PARMIGIANA!

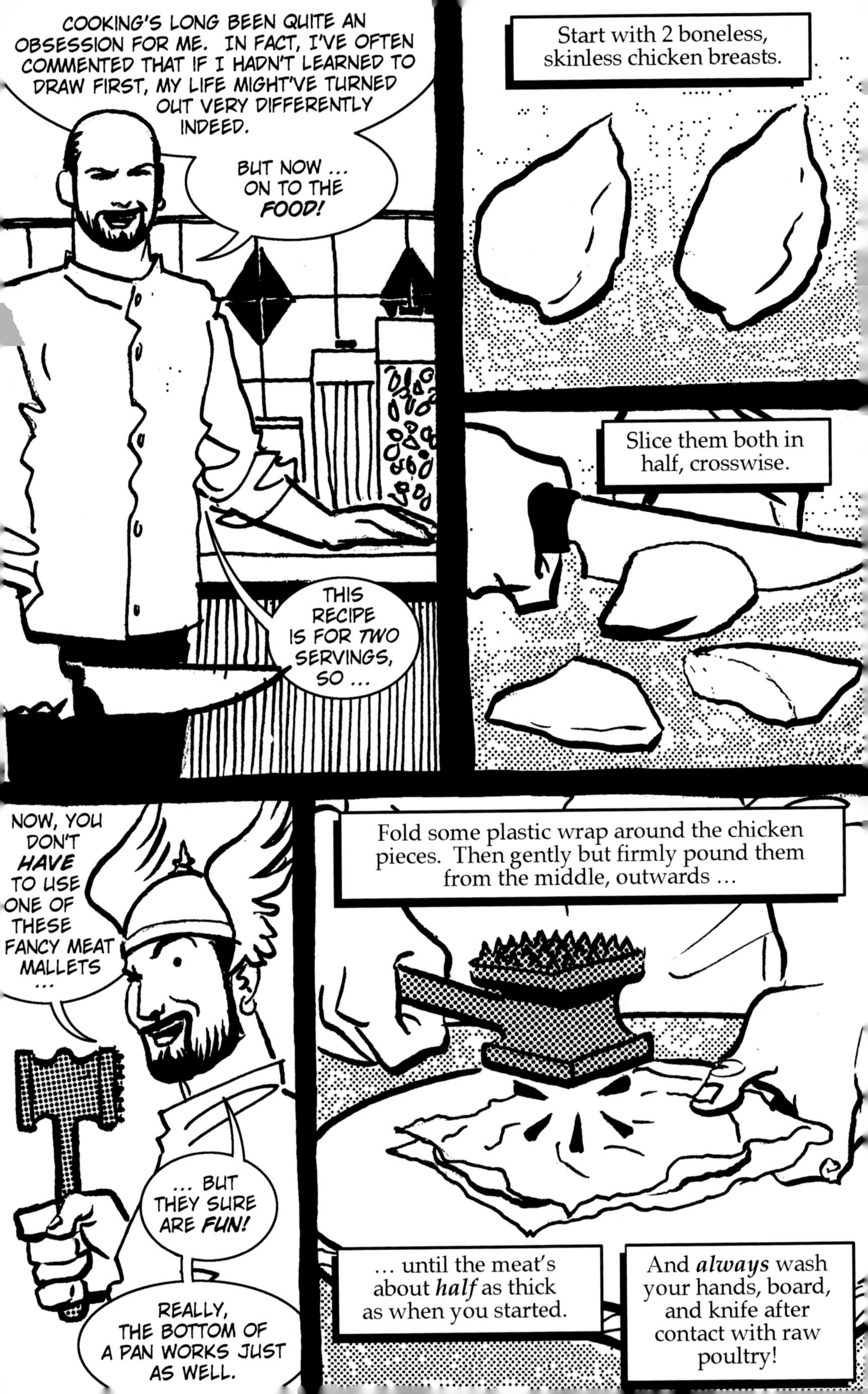
COOKING'S LONG BEEN QUITE AN OBSESSION FOR ME. IN FACT, I'VE OFTEN COMMENTED THAT IF I HADN'T LEARNED TO DRAW FIRST, MY LIFE MIGHT'VE TURNED OUT VERY DIFFERENTLY INDEED.
BUT NOW ... ON TO THE *FOOD!*
THIS RECIPE IS FOR *TWO* SERVINGS, SO ...
Start with 2 boneless, skinless chicken breasts.
Slice them both in half, crosswise.
NOW, YOU DON'T *HAVE* TO USE ONE OF THESE FANCY MEAT MALLETS ...
... BUT THEY SURE ARE *FUN!*
REALLY, THE BOTTOM OF A PAN WORKS JUST AS WELL.
Fold some plastic wrap around the chicken pieces. Then gently but firmly pound them from the middle, outwards ...
... until the meat's about *half* as thick as when you started.
And *always* wash your hands, board, and knife after contact with raw poultry!

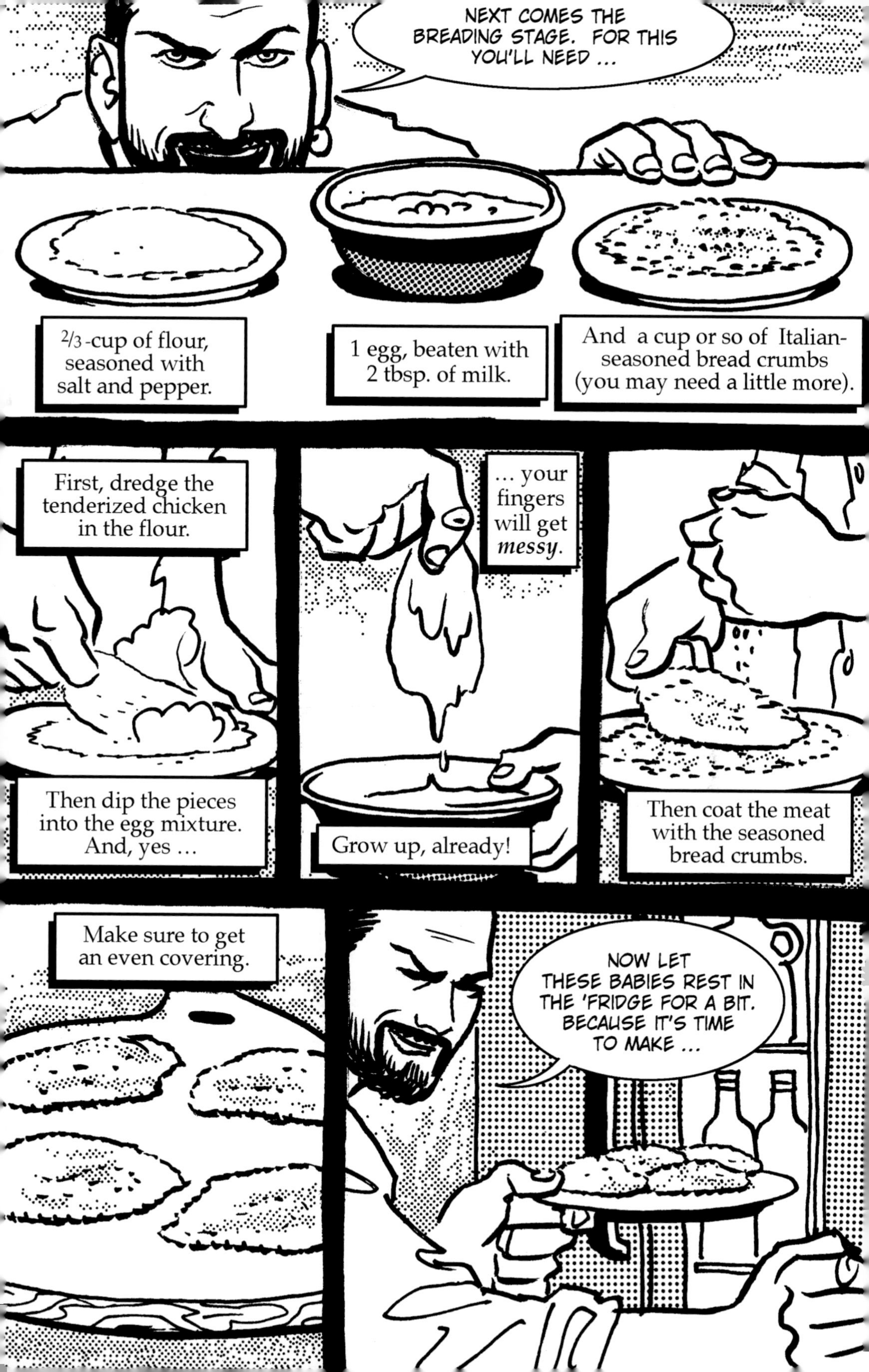
NEXT COMES THE BREADING STAGE. FOR THIS YOU'LL NEED ...
2/3-cup of flour, seasoned with salt and pepper.
1 egg, beaten with 2 tbsp. of milk.
And a cup or so of Italian-seasoned bread crumbs (you may need a little more).
First, dredge the tenderized chicken in the flour.
Then dip the pieces into the egg mixture. And, yes ...
... your fingers will get *messy*.
Grow up, already!
Then coat the meat with the seasoned bread crumbs.
Make sure to get an even covering.
NOW LET THESE BABIES REST IN THE 'FRIDGE FOR A BIT. BECAUSE IT'S TIME TO MAKE ...

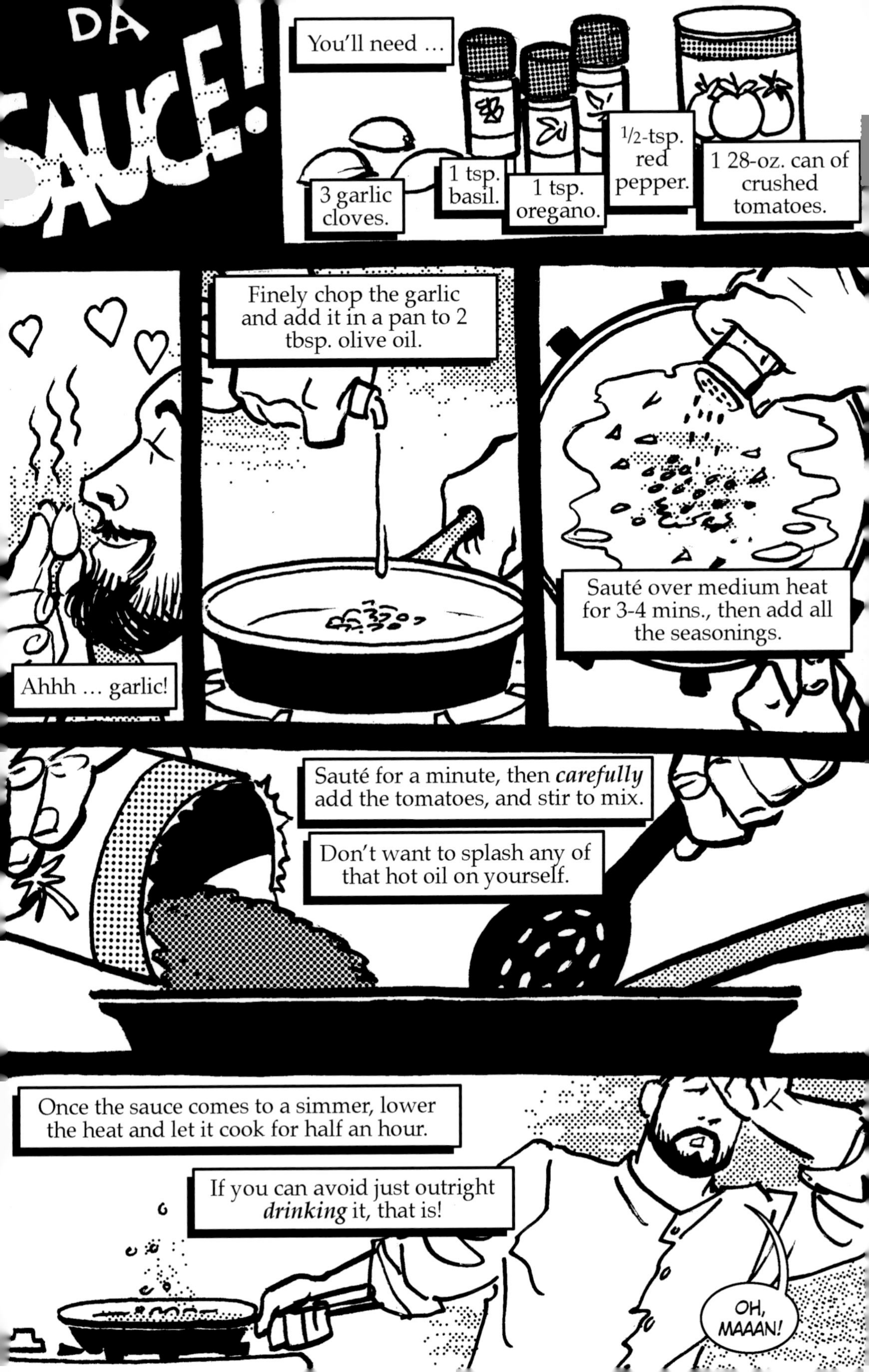
DA SAUCE!
You'll need ...
3 garlic cloves.
1 tsp. basil.
1 tsp. oregano.
$^1/_2$-tsp. red pepper.
1 28-oz. can of crushed tomatoes.
Ahhh ... garlic!
Finely chop the garlic and add it in a pan to 2 tbsp. olive oil.
Sauté over medium heat for 3-4 mins., then add all the seasonings.
Sauté for a minute, then *carefully* add the tomatoes, and stir to mix.
Don't want to splash any of that hot oil on yourself.
Once the sauce comes to a simmer, lower the heat and let it cook for half an hour.
If you can avoid just outright *drinking* it, that is!
OH, MAAAN!

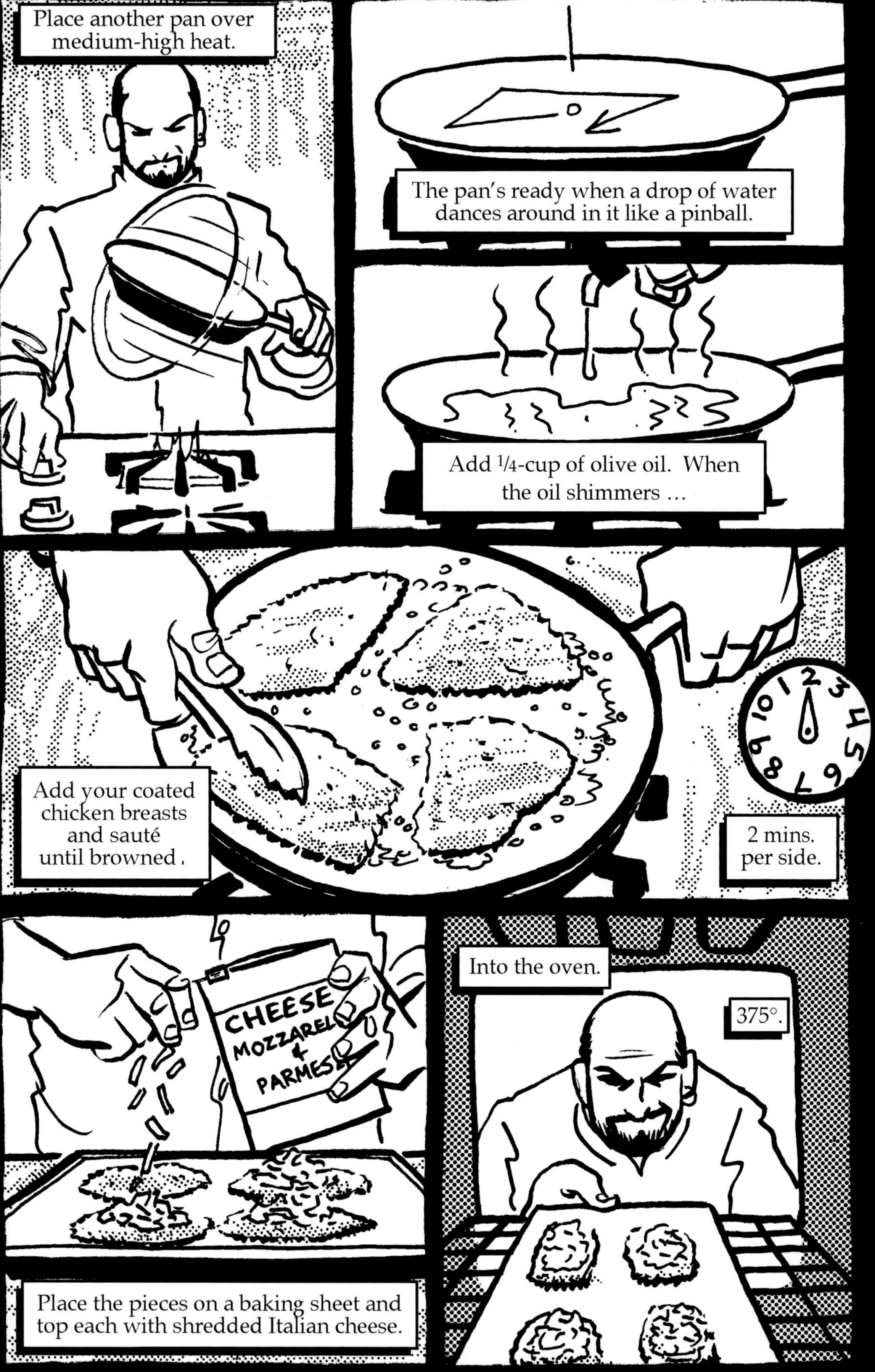
Place another pan over medium-high heat.
The pan's ready when a drop of water dances around in it like a pinball.
Add 1/4-cup of olive oil. When the oil shimmers …
Add your coated chicken breasts and sauté until browned.
2 mins. per side.
CHEESE
Place the pieces on a baking sheet and top each with shredded Italian cheese.
Into the oven.
375°.

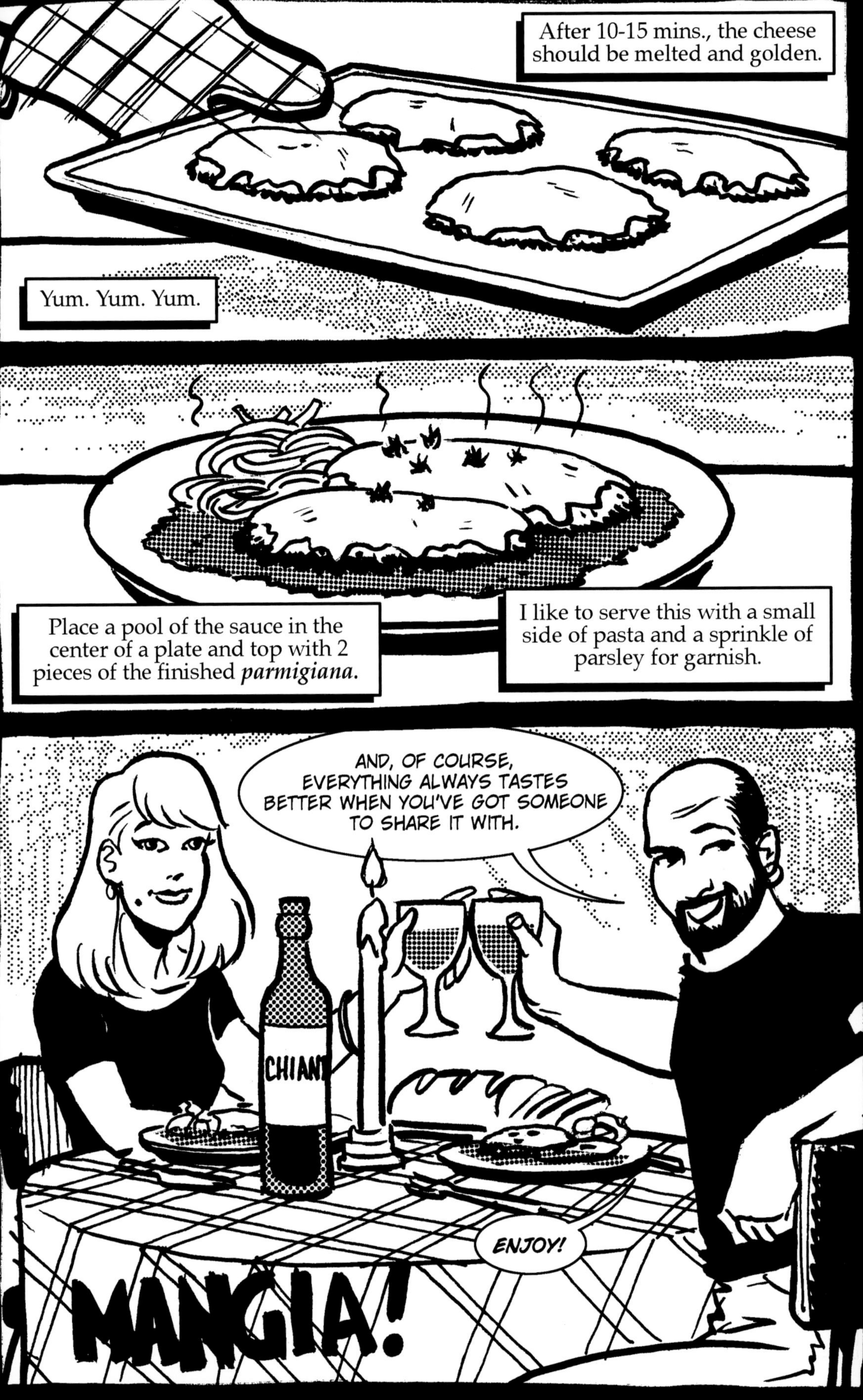
After 10-15 mins., the cheese should be melted and golden.
Yum. Yum. Yum.
Place a pool of the sauce in the center of a plate and top with 2 pieces of the finished *parmigiana*.
I like to serve this with a small side of pasta and a sprinkle of parsley for garnish.
AND, OF COURSE, EVERYTHING ALWAYS TASTES BETTER WHEN YOU'VE GOT SOMEONE TO SHARE IT WITH.
ENJOY!
MANGIA!

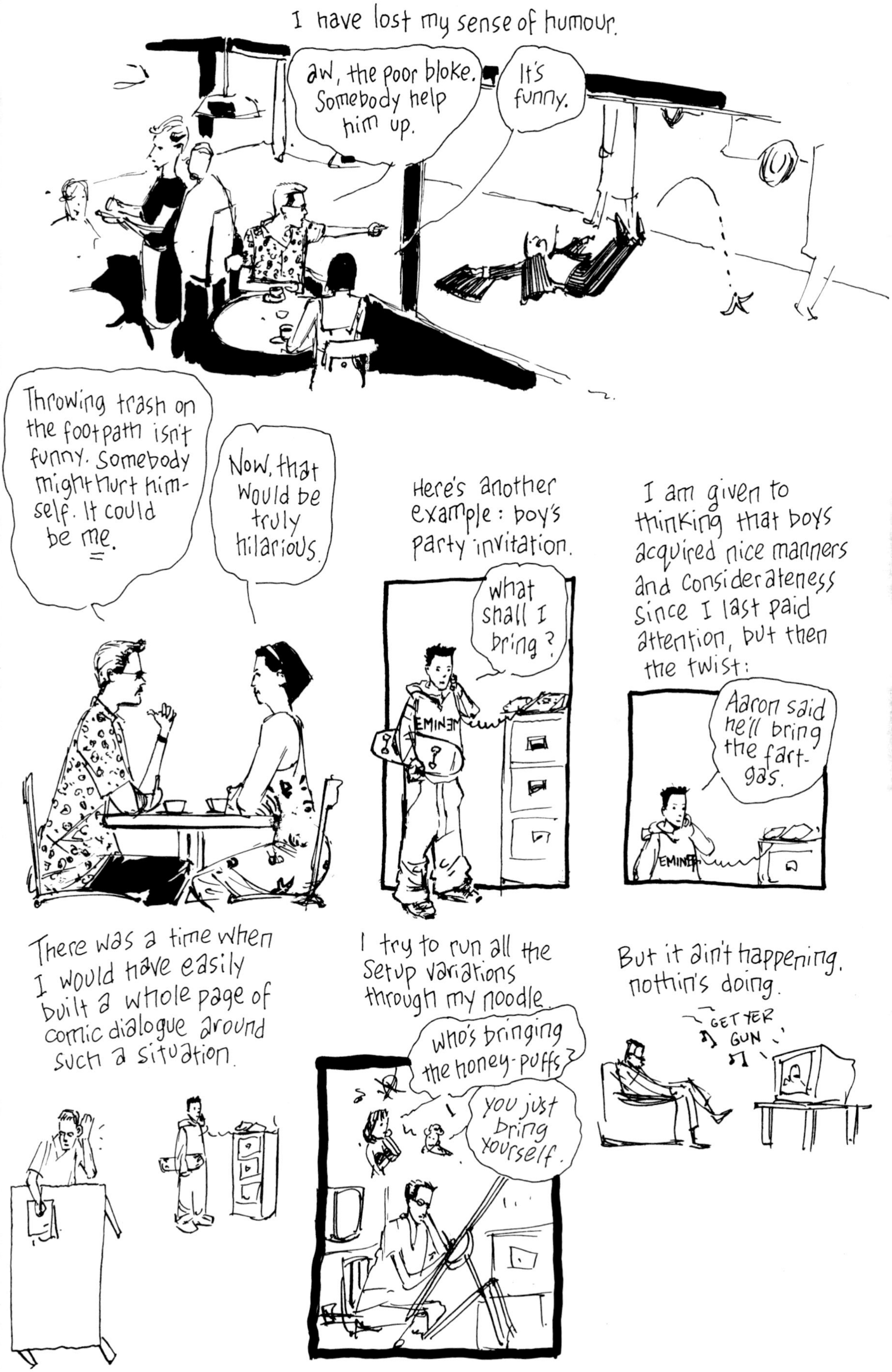
I have lost my sense of humour.
aw, the poor bloke. Somebody help him up.
It's funny.
Throwing trash on the footpath isn't funny. Somebody might hurt himself. It could be me.
Now, that would be truly hilarious.
Here's another example: boy's party invitation.
what shall I bring?
EMINEM
I am given to thinking that boys acquired nice manners and considerateness since I last paid attention, but then the twist:
Aaron said he'll bring the fart-gas.
EMINEM
There was a time when I would have easily built a whole page of comic dialogue around such a situation.
I try to run all the setup variations through my noodle.
who's bringing the honey-puffs?
you just bring yourself.
But it ain't happening. nothin's doing.
GET YER GUN

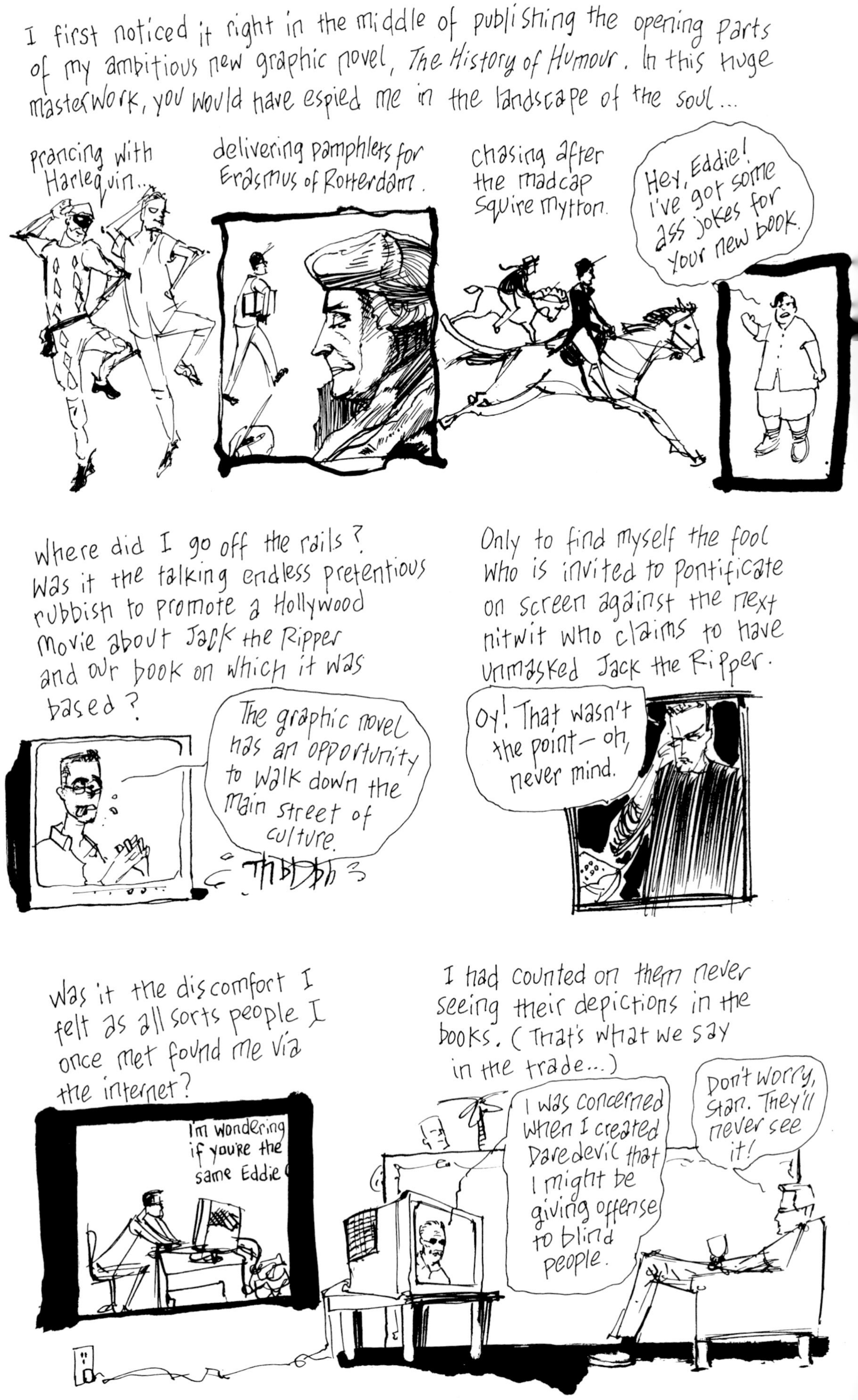
I first noticed it right in the middle of publishing the opening parts of my ambitious new graphic novel, *The History of Humour*. In this huge masterwork, you would have espied me in the landscape of the soul...
prancing with Harlequin...
delivering pamphlets for Erasmus of Rotterdam.
chasing after the madcap Squire Mytton.
Hey, Eddie! I've got some ass jokes for your new book.
Where did I go off the rails? Was it the talking endless pretentious rubbish to promote a Hollywood movie about Jack the Ripper and our book on which it was based?
The graphic novel has an opportunity to walk down the main street of culture.
THBBBH
Only to find myself the fool who is invited to pontificate on screen against the next nitwit who claims to have unmasked Jack the Ripper.
Oy! That wasn't the point— oh, never mind.
Was it the discomfort I felt as all sorts people I once met found me via the internet?
I'm wondering if you're the same Eddie
I had counted on them never seeing their depictions in the books. (That's what we say in the trade...)
I was concerned when I created Daredevil that I might be giving offense to blind people.
Don't worry, Stan. They'll never see it!

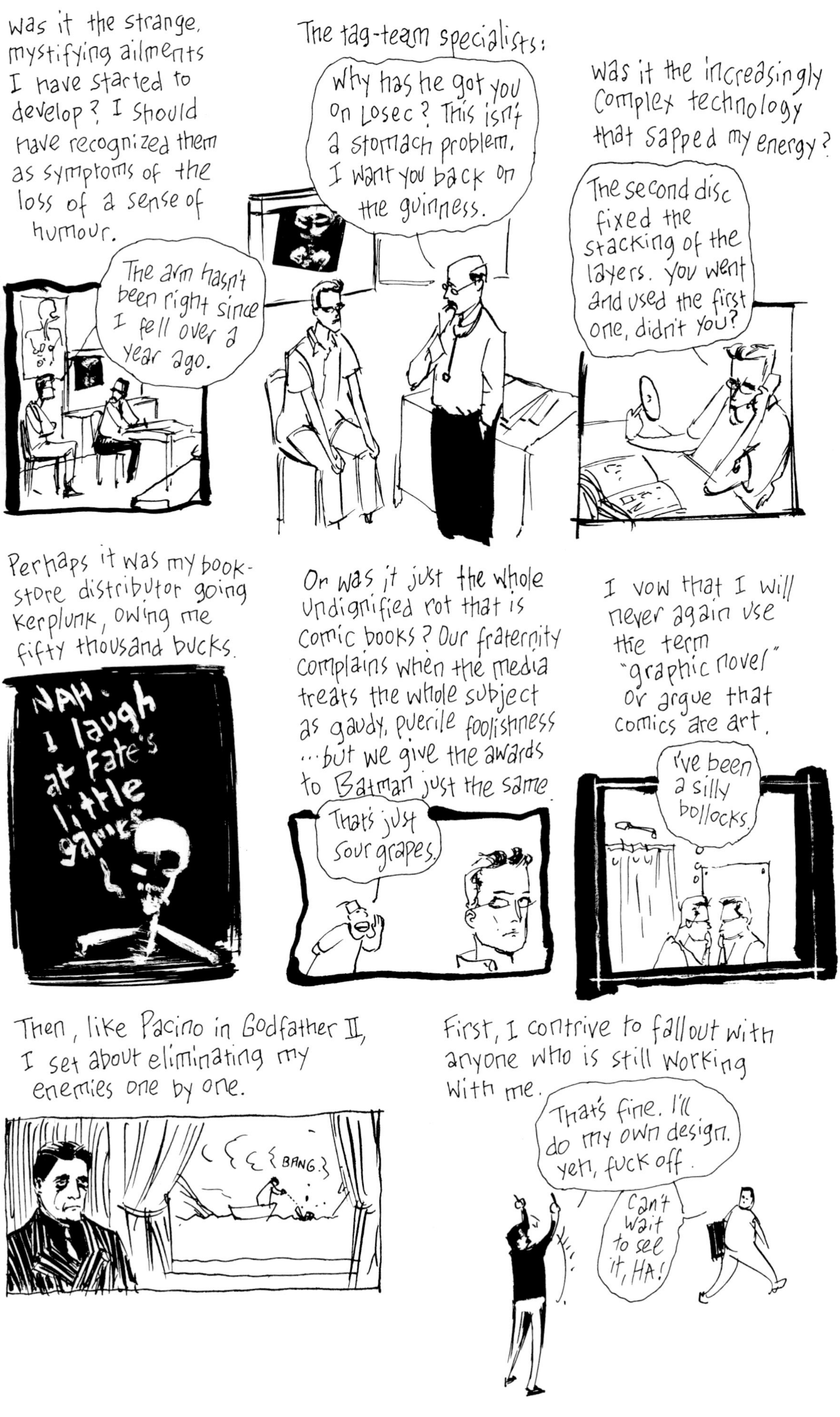

Was it the strange, mystifying ailments I have started to develop? I should have recognized them as symptoms of the loss of a sense of humour.
The arm hasn't been right since I fell over a year ago.
The tag-team specialists:
Why has he got you on Losec? This isn't a stomach problem. I want you back on the guinness.
Was it the increasingly complex technology that sapped my energy?
The second disc fixed the stacking of the layers. You went and used the first one, didn't you?
Perhaps it was my book-store distributor going kerplunk, owing me fifty thousand bucks.
NAH. I laugh at Fate's little games
Or was it just the whole undignified rot that is comic books? Our fraternity complains when the media treats the whole subject as gaudy, puerile foolishness ...but we give the awards to Batman just the same.
That's just sour grapes.
I vow that I will never again use the term "graphic novel" or argue that comics are art.
I've been a silly bollocks.
Then, like Pacino in Godfather II, I set about eliminating my enemies one by one.
BANG.
First, I contrive to fall out with anyone who is still working with me.
That's fine. I'll do my own design. Yeh, fuck off.
Can't wait to see it, HA!

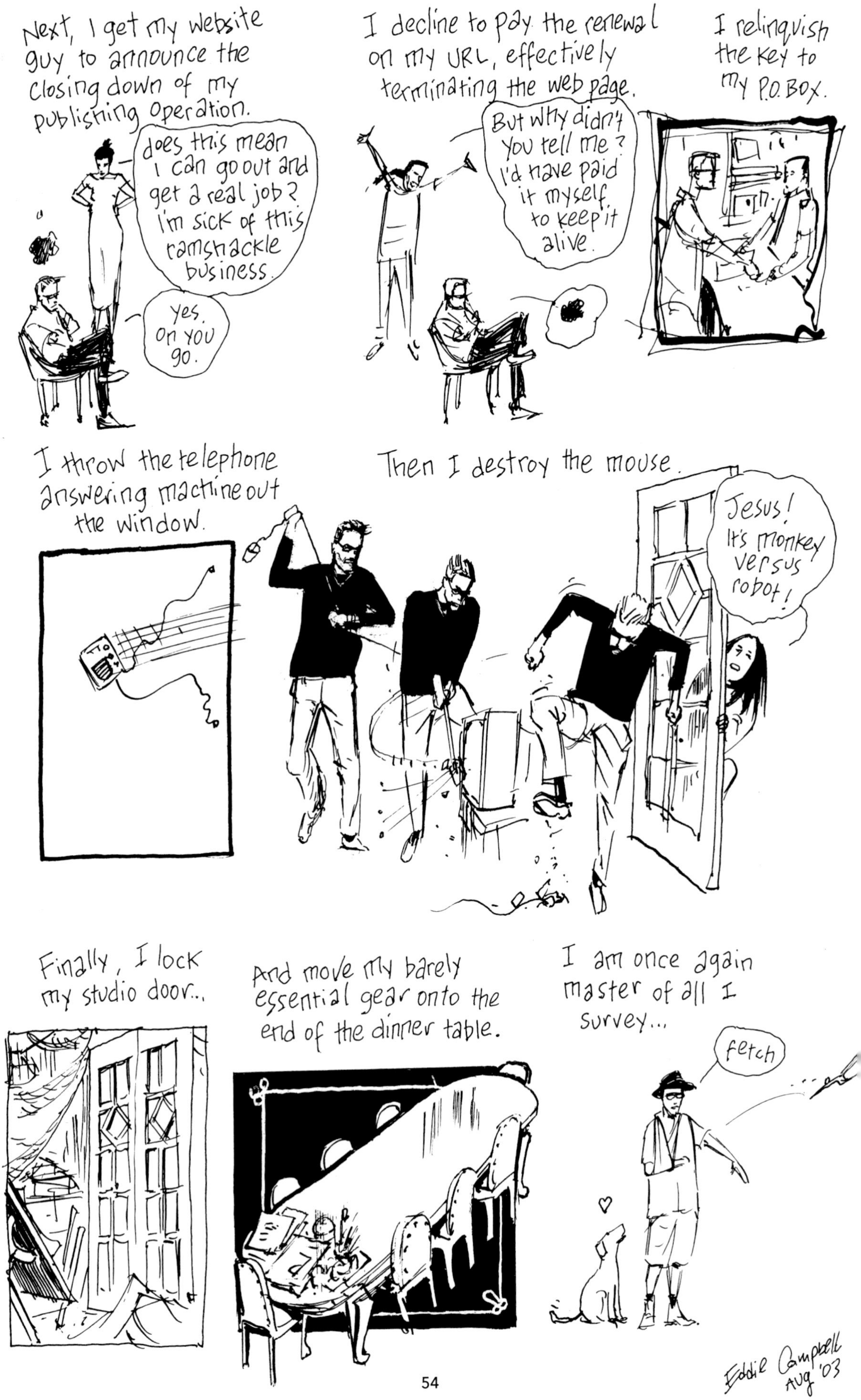
Next, I get my website guy to announce the closing down of my publishing operation.
does this mean I can go out and get a real job? I'm sick of this ramshackle business.
yes. on you go.
I decline to pay the renewal on my URL, effectively terminating the web page.
But why didn't you tell me? I'd have paid it myself to keep it alive.
I relinquish the key to my P.O. BOX.
I throw the telephone answering machine out the window.
Then I destroy the mouse.
Jesus! It's monkey versus robot!
Finally, I lock my studio door...
And move my barely essential gear onto the end of the dinner table.
I am once again master of all I survey...
fetch
Eddie Campbell Aug '03

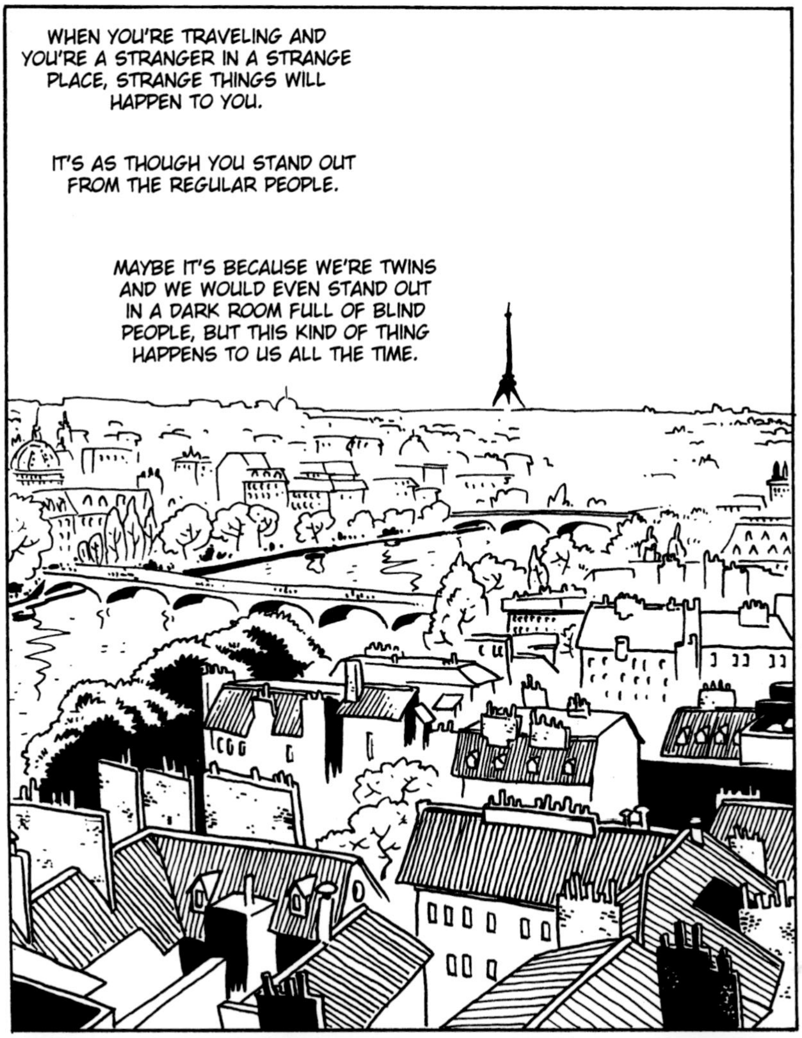
WHEN YOU'RE TRAVELING AND YOU'RE A STRANGER IN A STRANGE PLACE, STRANGE THINGS WILL HAPPEN TO YOU.
IT'S AS THOUGH YOU STAND OUT FROM THE REGULAR PEOPLE.
MAYBE IT'S BECAUSE WE'RE TWINS AND WE WOULD EVEN STAND OUT IN A DARK ROOM FULL OF BLIND PEOPLE, BUT THIS KIND OF THING HAPPENS TO US ALL THE TIME.

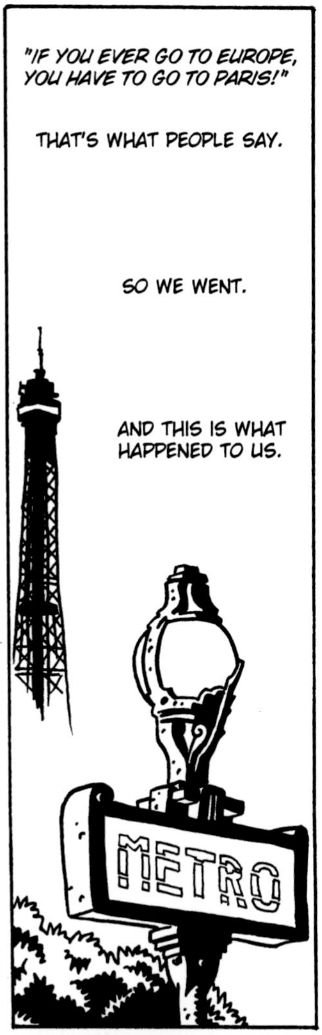
"IF YOU EVER GO TO EUROPE, YOU HAVE TO GO TO PARIS!"
THAT'S WHAT PEOPLE SAY.
SO WE WENT.
AND THIS IS WHAT HAPPENED TO US.
METRO

qu'est-ce que c'est?

Fábio Moon Gabriel Bá

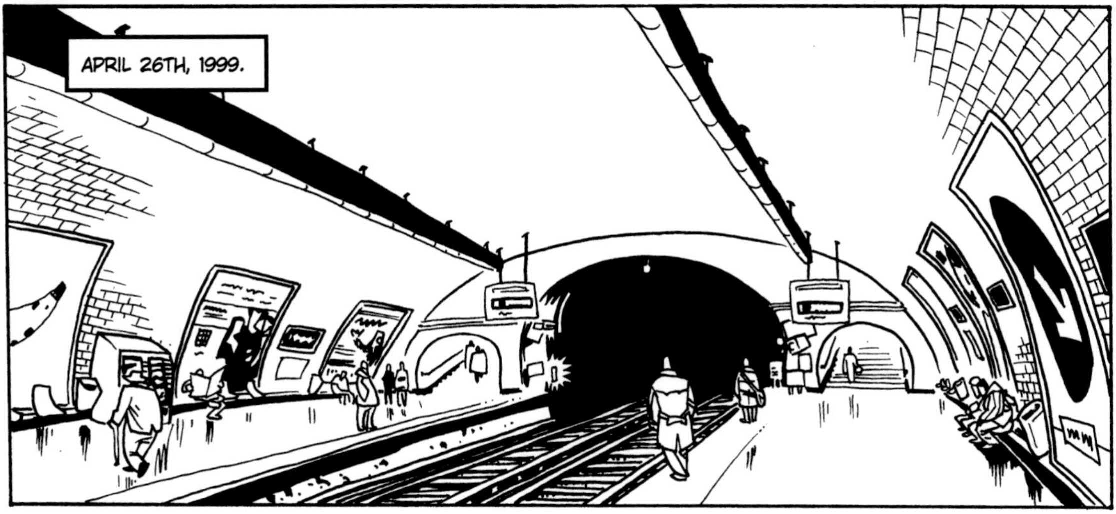
APRIL 26TH, 1999.

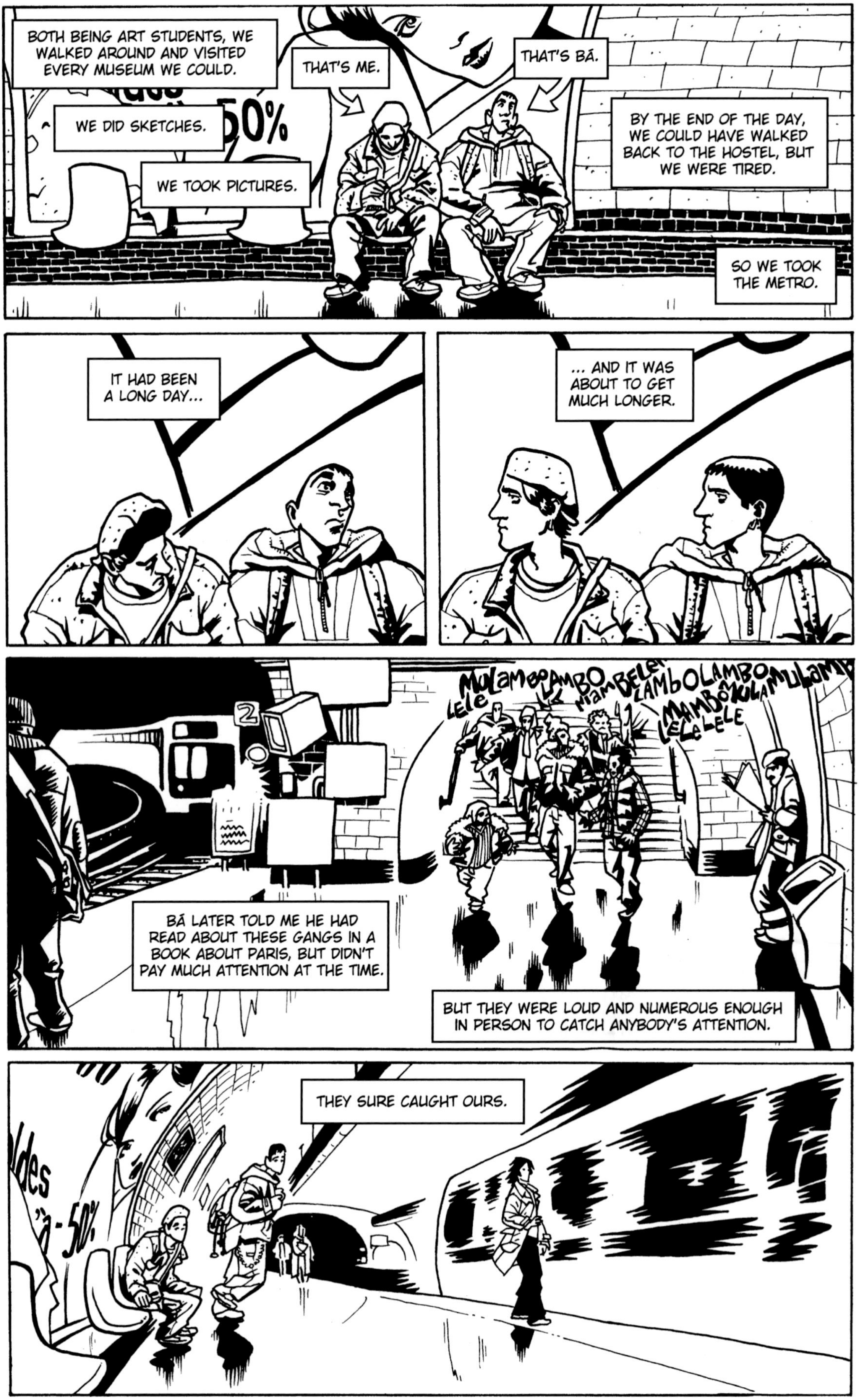
BOTH BEING ART STUDENTS, WE WALKED AROUND AND VISITED EVERY MUSEUM WE COULD.
WE DID SKETCHES.
WE TOOK PICTURES.
THAT'S ME.
THAT'S BÁ.
BY THE END OF THE DAY, WE COULD HAVE WALKED BACK TO THE HOSTEL, BUT WE WERE TIRED.
SO WE TOOK THE METRO.
IT HAD BEEN A LONG DAY...
... AND IT WAS ABOUT TO GET MUCH LONGER.
MULAMBOLAMBO
LELE
MAMBELE
LAMBOLAMBO
MAMBOKULA
LELELELE
BÁ LATER TOLD ME HE HAD READ ABOUT THESE GANGS IN A BOOK ABOUT PARIS, BUT DIDN'T PAY MUCH ATTENTION AT THE TIME.
BUT THEY WERE LOUD AND NUMEROUS ENOUGH IN PERSON TO CATCH ANYBODY'S ATTENTION.
THEY SURE CAUGHT OURS.

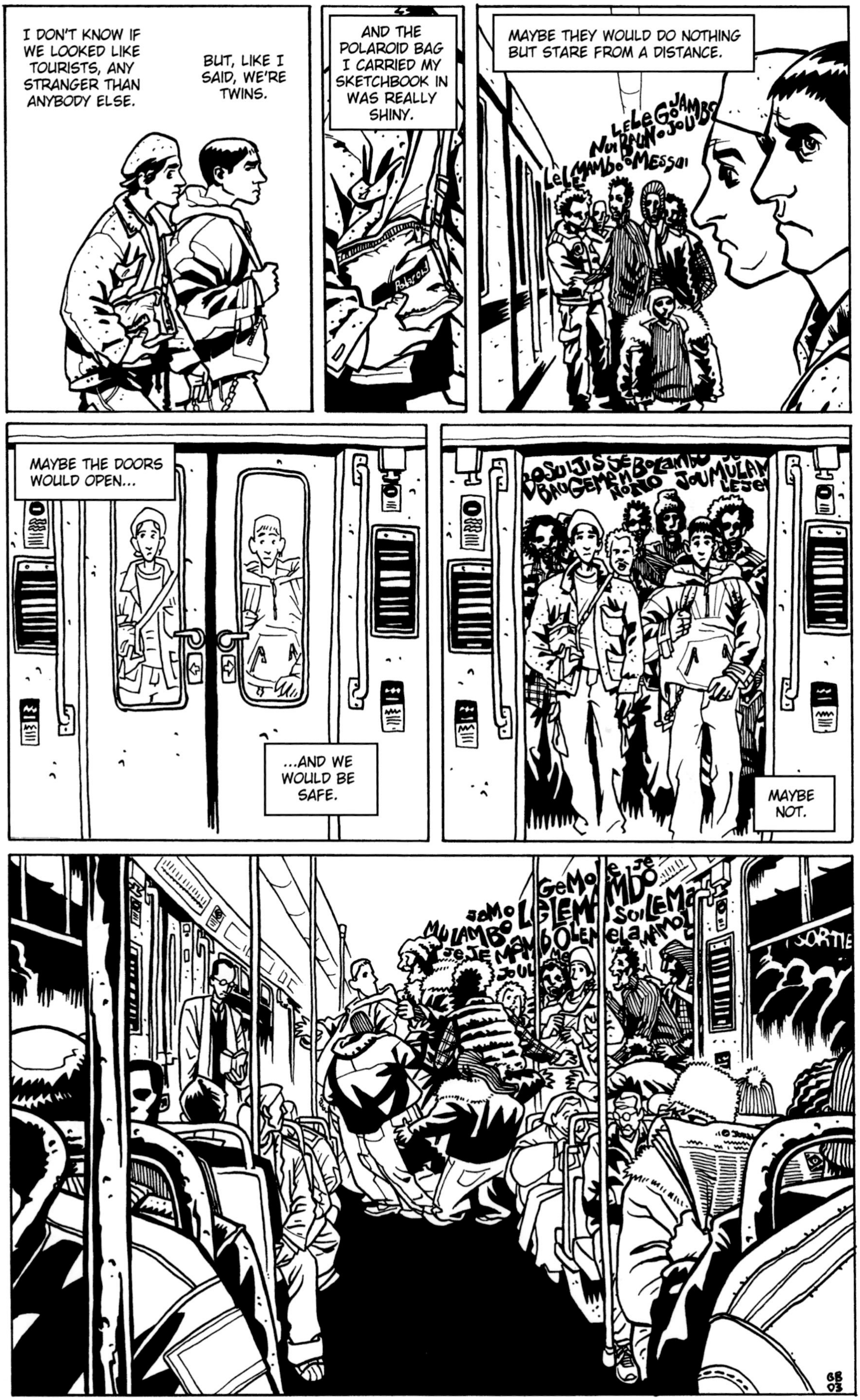
I DON'T KNOW IF WE LOOKED LIKE TOURISTS, ANY STRANGER THAN ANYBODY ELSE.
BUT, LIKE I SAID, WE'RE TWINS.
AND THE POLAROID BAG I CARRIED MY SKETCHBOOK IN WAS REALLY SHINY.
Polaroid
MAYBE THEY WOULD DO NOTHING BUT STARE FROM A DISTANCE.
MAYBE THE DOORS WOULD OPEN...
...AND WE WOULD BE SAFE.
MAYBE NOT.
SORTIE
GB 03

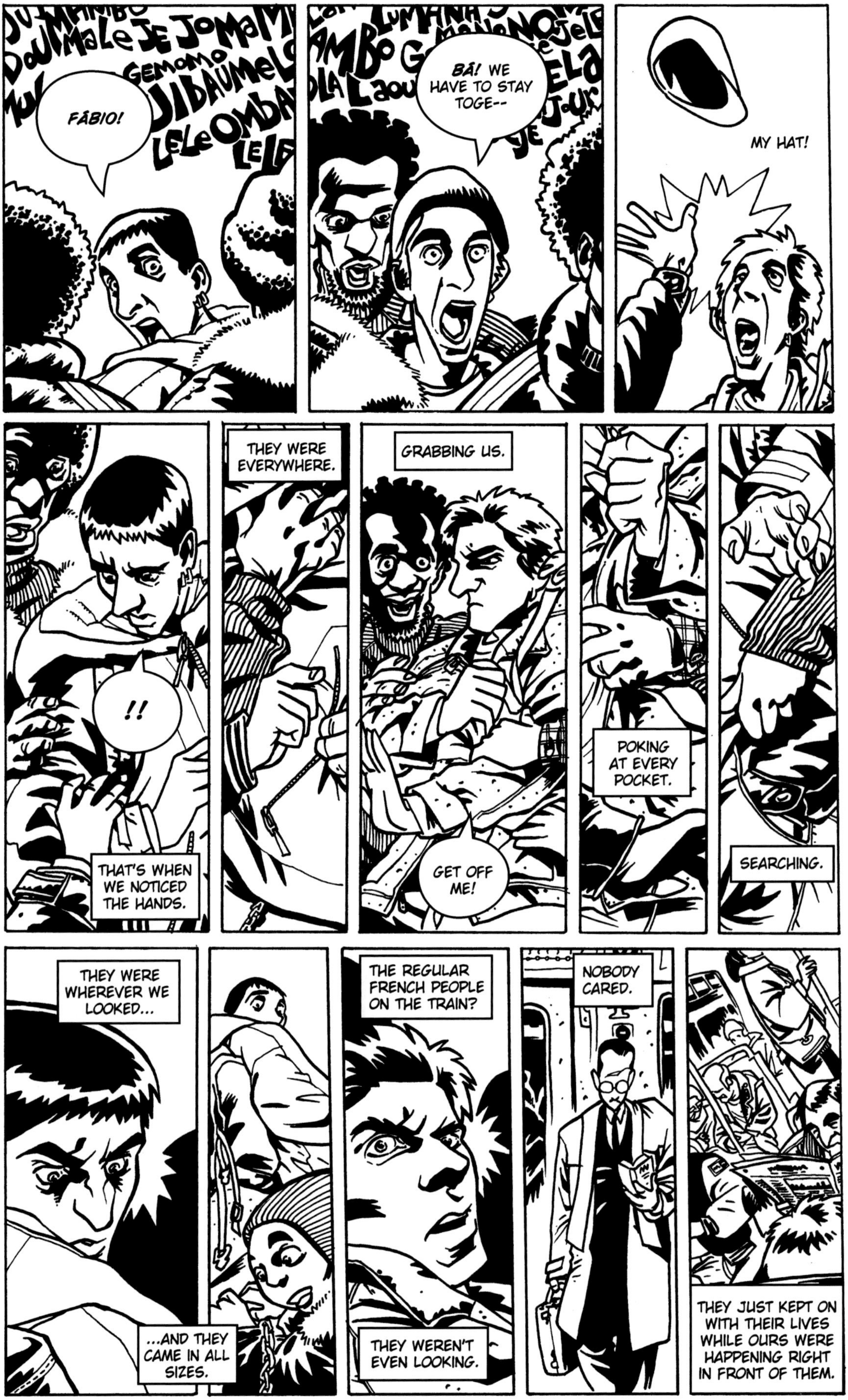
FÁBIO!
BÁ! WE HAVE TO STAY TOGE--
MY HAT!
THAT'S WHEN WE NOTICED THE HANDS.
!!
THEY WERE EVERYWHERE.
GRABBING US.
GET OFF ME!
POKING AT EVERY POCKET.
SEARCHING.
THEY WERE WHEREVER WE LOOKED...
...AND THEY CAME IN ALL SIZES.
THE REGULAR FRENCH PEOPLE ON THE TRAIN?
THEY WEREN'T EVEN LOOKING.
NOBODY CARED.
THEY JUST KEPT ON WITH THEIR LIVES WHILE OURS WERE HAPPENING RIGHT IN FRONT OF THEM.

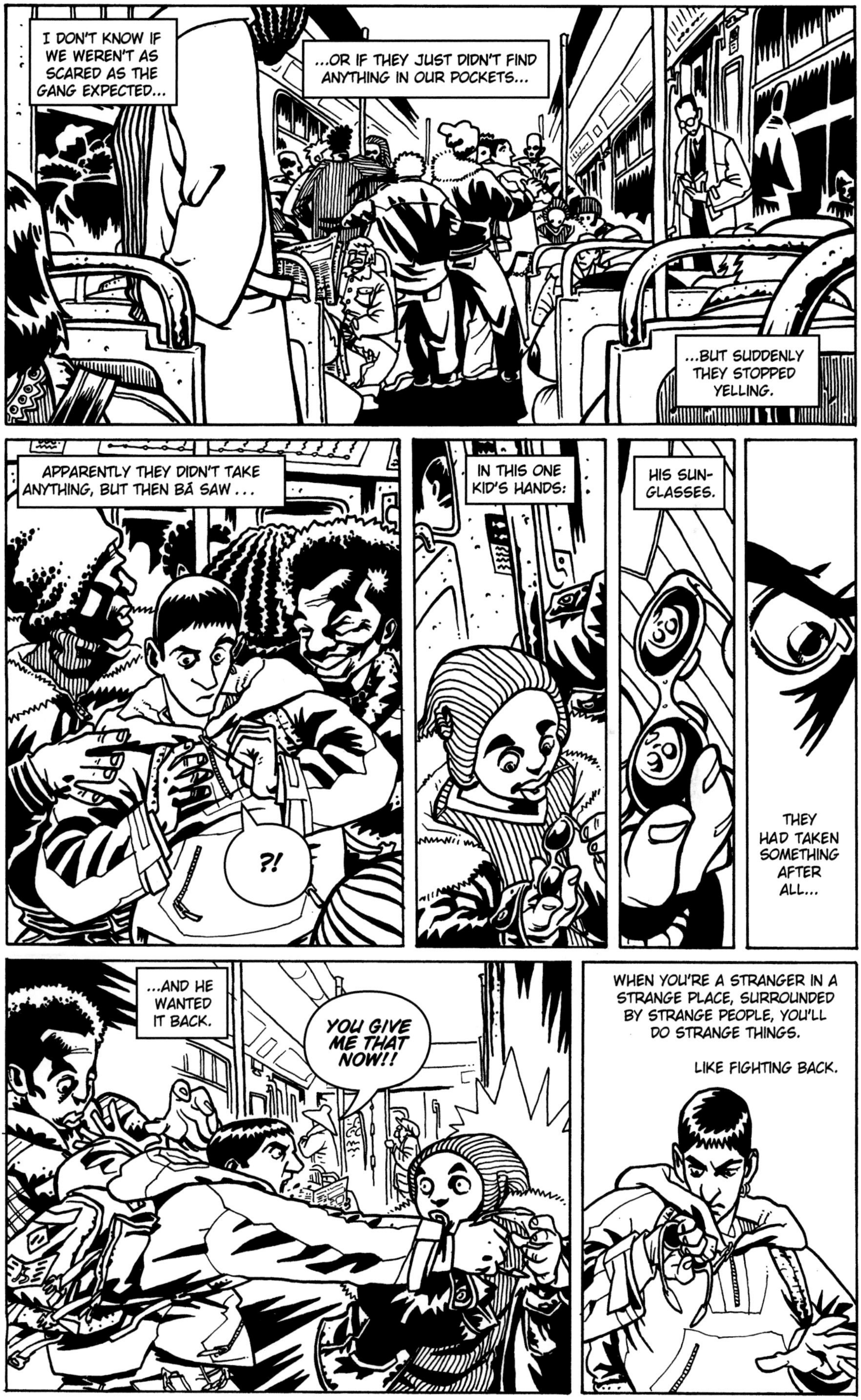
I DON'T KNOW IF WE WEREN'T AS SCARED AS THE GANG EXPECTED...
...OR IF THEY JUST DIDN'T FIND ANYTHING IN OUR POCKETS...
...BUT SUDDENLY THEY STOPPED YELLING.
APPARENTLY THEY DIDN'T TAKE ANYTHING, BUT THEN BÁ SAW . . .
?!
IN THIS ONE KID'S HANDS:
HIS SUN-GLASSES.
THEY HAD TAKEN SOMETHING AFTER ALL...
...AND HE WANTED IT BACK.
YOU GIVE ME THAT NOW!!
WHEN YOU'RE A STRANGER IN A STRANGE PLACE, SURROUNDED BY STRANGE PEOPLE, YOU'LL DO STRANGE THINGS.
LIKE FIGHTING BACK.

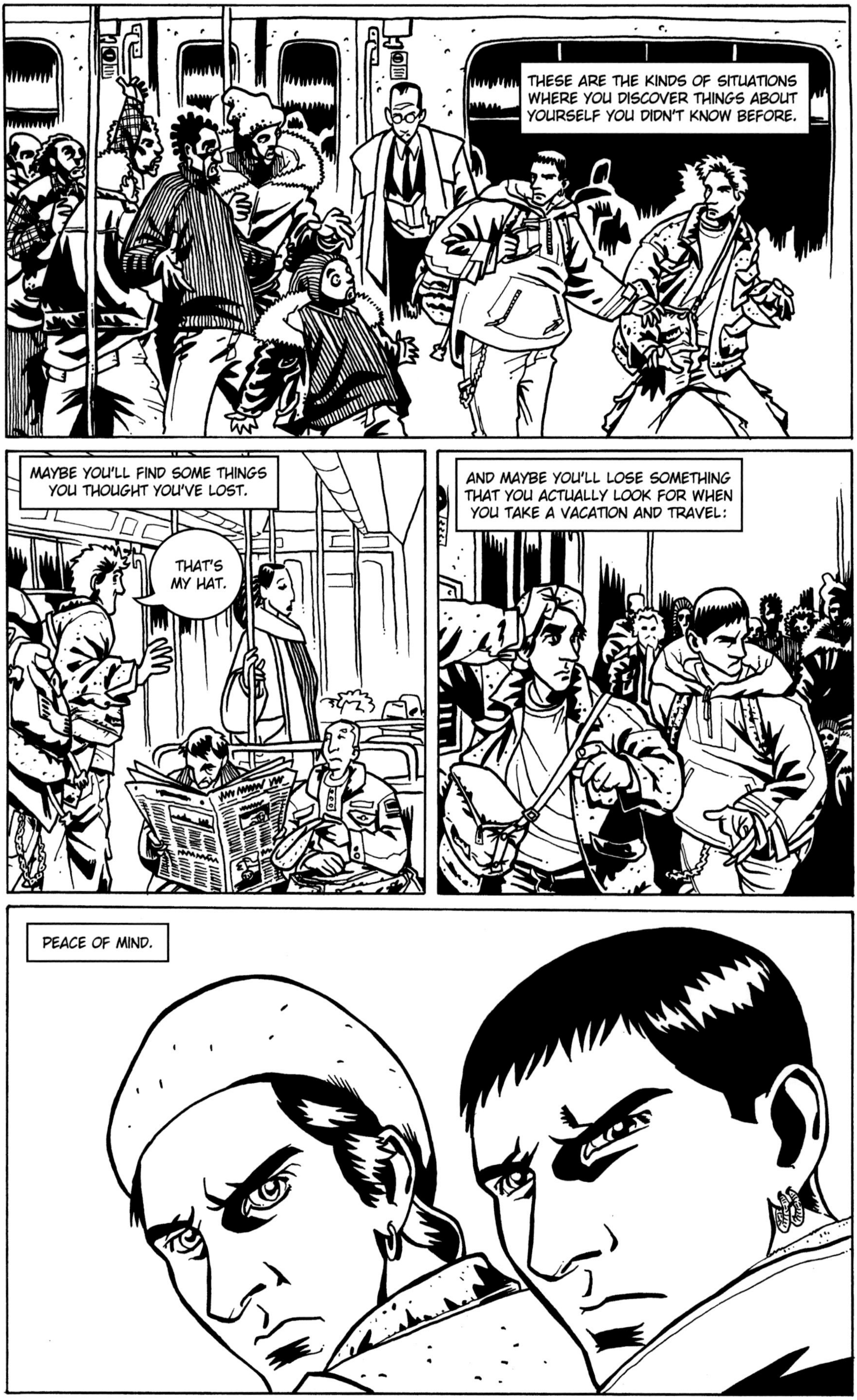
THESE ARE THE KINDS OF SITUATIONS WHERE YOU DISCOVER THINGS ABOUT YOURSELF YOU DIDN'T KNOW BEFORE.
MAYBE YOU'LL FIND SOME THINGS YOU THOUGHT YOU'VE LOST.
THAT'S MY HAT.
AND MAYBE YOU'LL LOSE SOMETHING THAT YOU ACTUALLY LOOK FOR WHEN YOU TAKE A VACATION AND TRAVEL:
PEACE OF MIND.

TWO MORE STATIONS PASSED AND NOTHING HAPPENED.

IT WAS LIKE THEY WERE WAITING FOR US.

WHAT WOULD THEY DO WHEN WE FINALLY GOT TO OUR DESTINATION?

WHAT WOULD *WE* DO?

WOULD WE REALLY HAVE TO FIGHT OUR WAY OUT?

RUN FOR OUR LIVES?

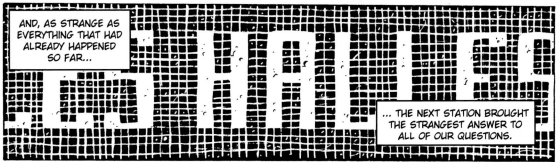

AND, AS STRANGE AS EVERYTHING THAT HAD ALREADY HAPPENED SO FAR...

... THE NEXT STATION BROUGHT THE STRANGEST ANSWER TO ALL OF OUR QUESTIONS.

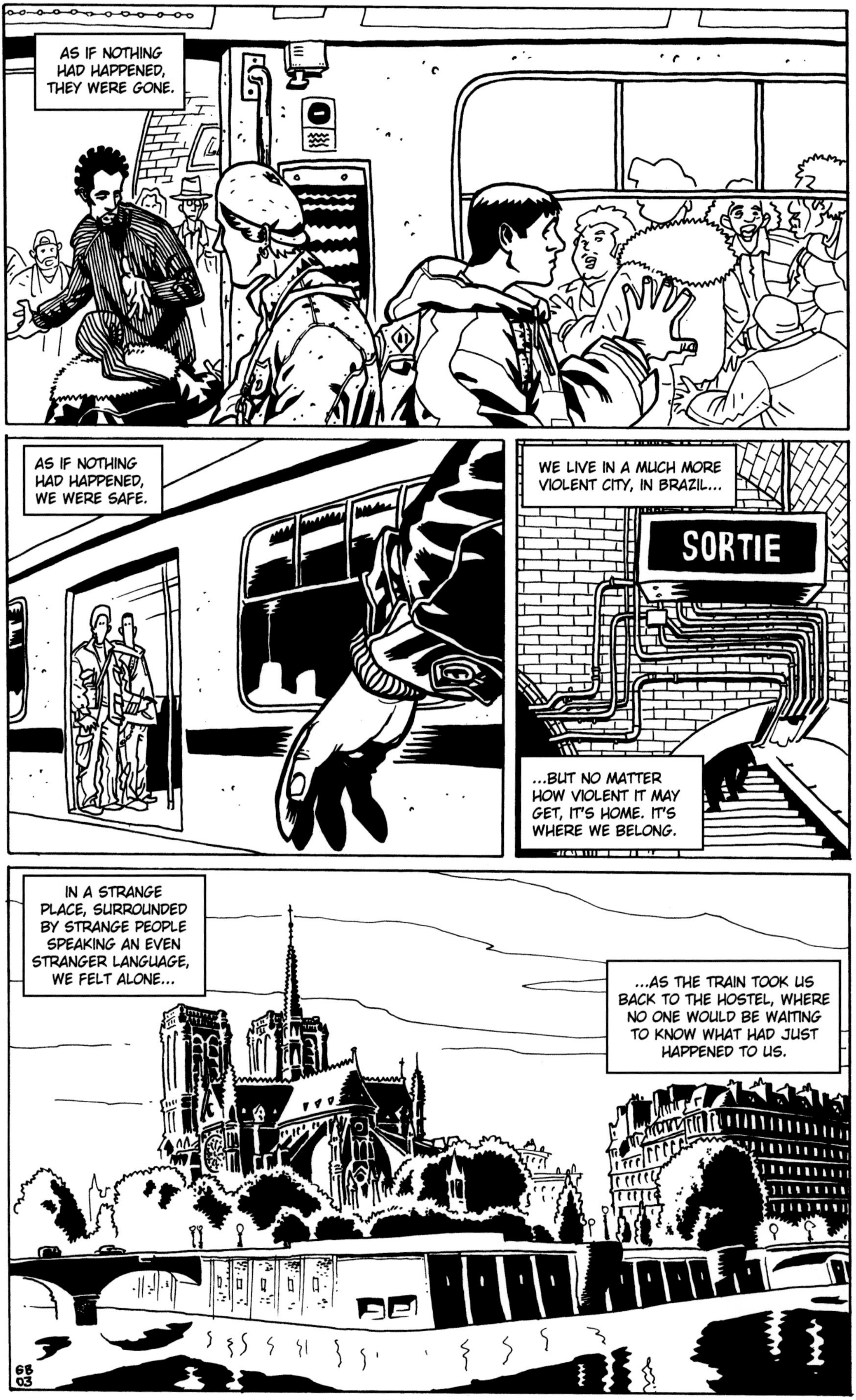
AS IF NOTHING HAD HAPPENED, THEY WERE GONE.
AS IF NOTHING HAD HAPPENED, WE WERE SAFE.
WE LIVE IN A MUCH MORE VIOLENT CITY, IN BRAZIL...
SORTIE
...BUT NO MATTER HOW VIOLENT IT MAY GET, IT'S HOME. IT'S WHERE WE BELONG.
IN A STRANGE PLACE, SURROUNDED BY STRANGE PEOPLE SPEAKING AN EVEN STRANGER LANGUAGE, WE FELT ALONE...
...AS THE TRAIN TOOK US BACK TO THE HOSTEL, WHERE NO ONE WOULD BE WAITING TO KNOW WHAT HAD JUST HAPPENED TO US.
GB 03

FRANCE

IT'S ANOTHER SAKAI TRAVEL REPORT!

JANUARY 23– FEBRUARY 1, 2002

IF FRANCE IS THE COMICS CENTER OF EUROPE, THEN ANGOULÊME, WITH ITS MUSEUM AND CARTOONING SCHOOL, IS ITS CAPITAL.

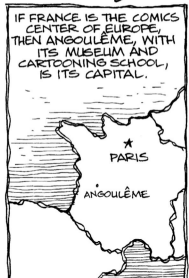

★ PARIS

ANGOULÊME

I ATTENDED THE *FESTIVAL de la BANDE DESSINEE ANGOULÊME* AS A GUEST OF MY FRENCH PUBLISHER, EDITIONS PAQUET.

SHARON, MY WIFE AND FAVORITE TRAVELING COMPANION, ACCOMPANIED ME. IT WAS ALSO OUR 25TH WEDDING ANNIVERSARY, AND WHERE BETTER TO CELEBRATE IT THAN FRANCE?

WE FLEW OUT OF LOS ANGELES EARLY WEDNESDAY MORNING, AND ARRIVED AT CHARLES DeGAULLE AIRPORT EARLY THURSDAY...

...TOOK THE AIR FRANCE BUS INTO PARIS...

...AND CAUGHT THE HIGH-SPEED TGV TRAIN TO ANGOULÊME.

ANGOULÊME IS A SMALL TOWN BUILT AROUND A 12TH CENTURY CATHEDRAL AT THE TOP OF A HILL.

WE HAD BEEN CAUTIONED TO EXPECT RAIN AND COLD, BUT THE WEATHER WAS VERY MILD. SUNLIGHT EVEN PEEKED THROUGH THE CLOUDS--AND IT ONLY GOT BETTER.

1

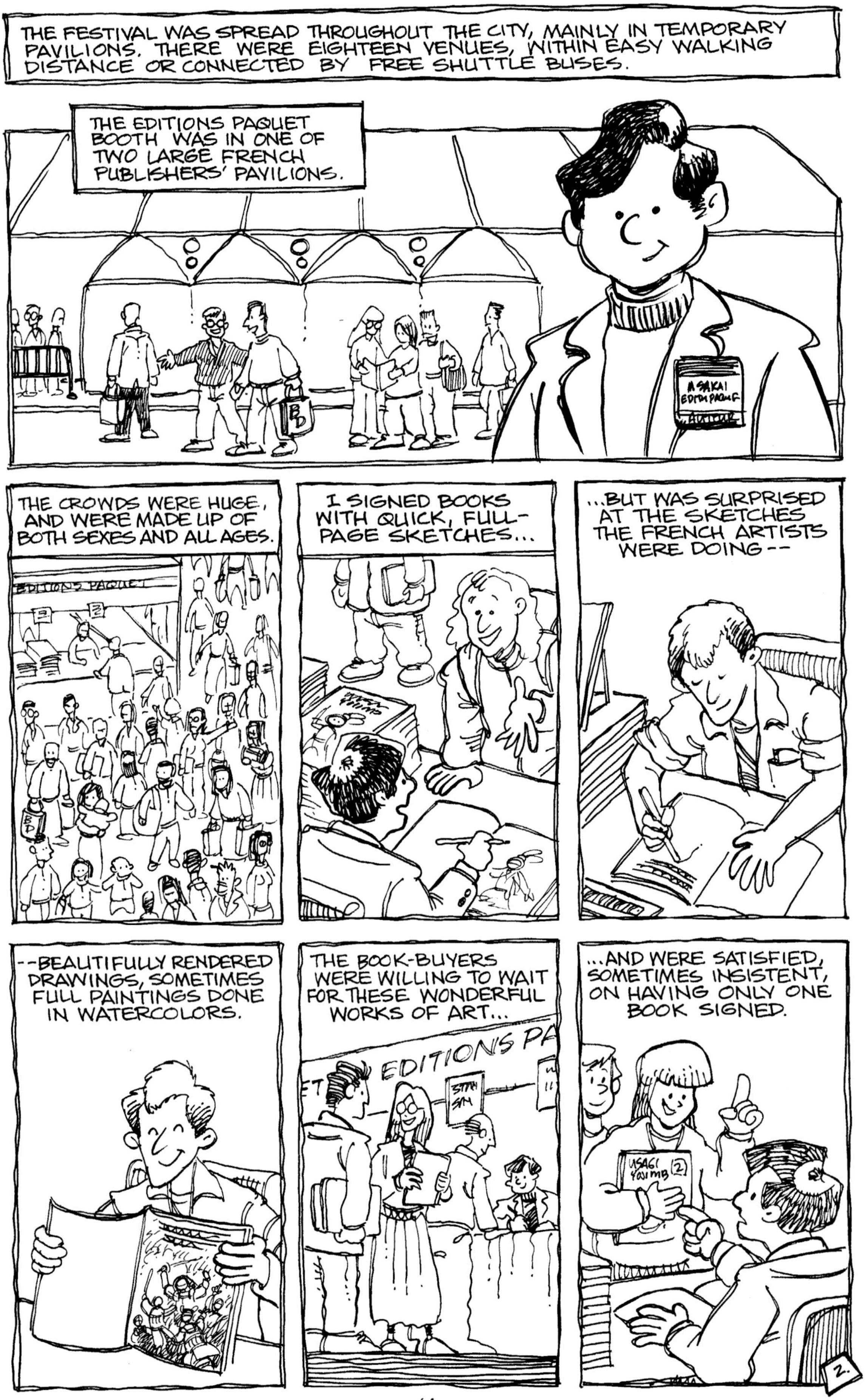
THE FESTIVAL WAS SPREAD THROUGHOUT THE CITY, MAINLY IN TEMPORARY PAVILIONS. THERE WERE EIGHTEEN VENUES, WITHIN EASY WALKING DISTANCE OR CONNECTED BY FREE SHUTTLE BUSES.
THE EDITIONS PAQUET BOOTH WAS IN ONE OF TWO LARGE FRENCH PUBLISHERS' PAVILIONS.
THE CROWDS WERE HUGE, AND WERE MADE UP OF BOTH SEXES AND ALL AGES.
I SIGNED BOOKS WITH QUICK, FULL-PAGE SKETCHES...
...BUT WAS SURPRISED AT THE SKETCHES THE FRENCH ARTISTS WERE DOING--
--BEAUTIFULLY RENDERED DRAWINGS, SOMETIMES FULL PAINTINGS DONE IN WATERCOLORS.
THE BOOK-BUYERS WERE WILLING TO WAIT FOR THESE WONDERFUL WORKS OF ART...
...AND WERE SATISFIED, SOMETIMES INSISTENT, ON HAVING ONLY ONE BOOK SIGNED.
2.

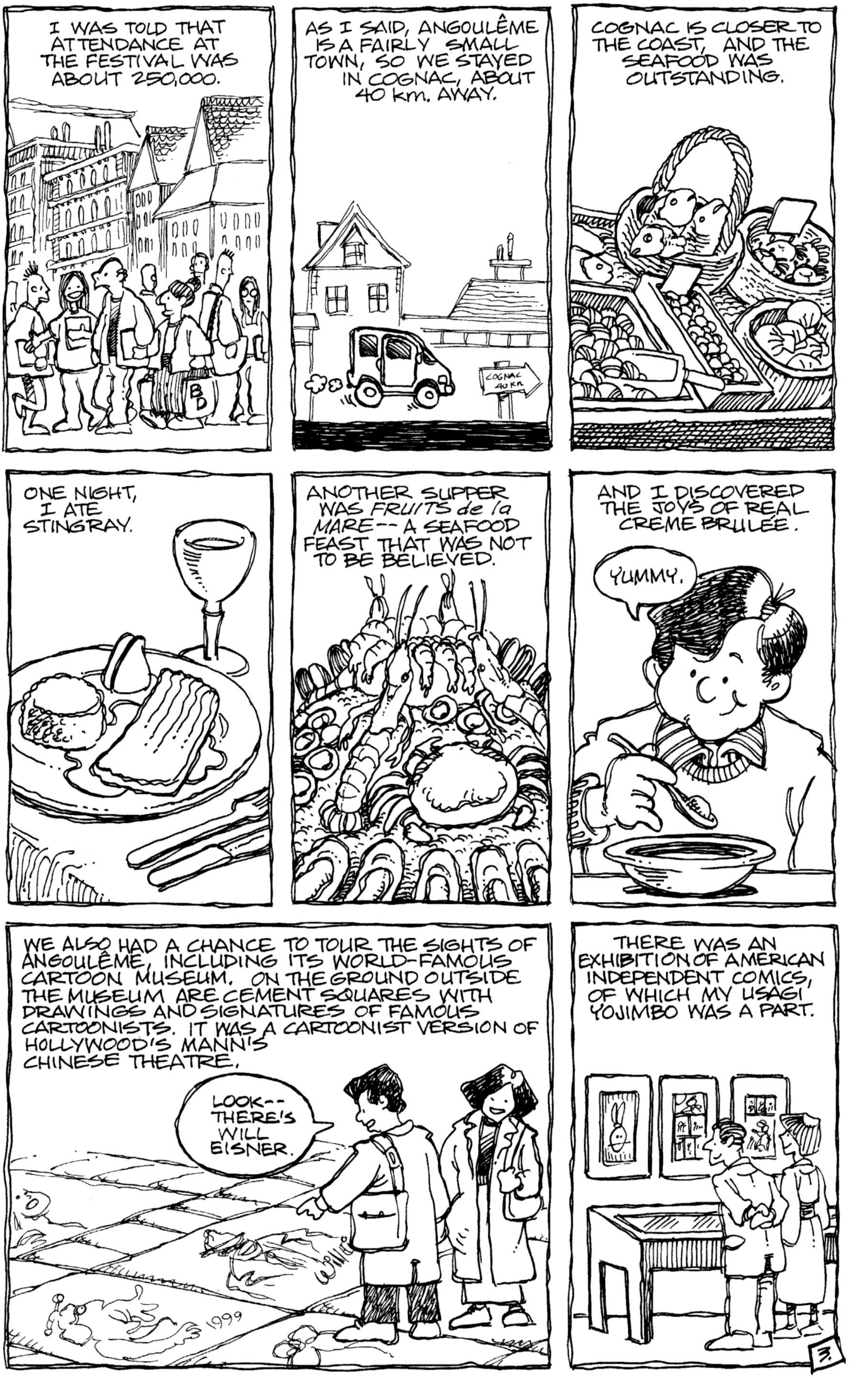
I WAS TOLD THAT ATTENDANCE AT THE FESTIVAL WAS ABOUT 250,000.
BD
AS I SAID, ANGOULÊME IS A FAIRLY SMALL TOWN, SO WE STAYED IN COGNAC, ABOUT 40 km. AWAY.
COGNAC 40 Km
COGNAC IS CLOSER TO THE COAST, AND THE SEAFOOD WAS OUTSTANDING.
ONE NIGHT, I ATE STINGRAY.
ANOTHER SUPPER WAS *FRUITS de la MARE*-- A SEAFOOD FEAST THAT WAS NOT TO BE BELIEVED.
AND I DISCOVERED THE JOYS OF REAL CREME BRULEE.
YUMMY.
WE ALSO HAD A CHANCE TO TOUR THE SIGHTS OF ANGOULÊME, INCLUDING ITS WORLD-FAMOUS CARTOON MUSEUM. ON THE GROUND OUTSIDE THE MUSEUM ARE CEMENT SQUARES WITH DRAWINGS AND SIGNATURES OF FAMOUS CARTOONISTS. IT WAS A CARTOONIST VERSION OF HOLLYWOOD'S MANN'S CHINESE THEATRE.
LOOK-- THERE'S WILL EISNER.
1999
THERE WAS AN EXHIBITION OF AMERICAN INDEPENDENT COMICS, OF WHICH MY USAGI YOJIMBO WAS A PART.

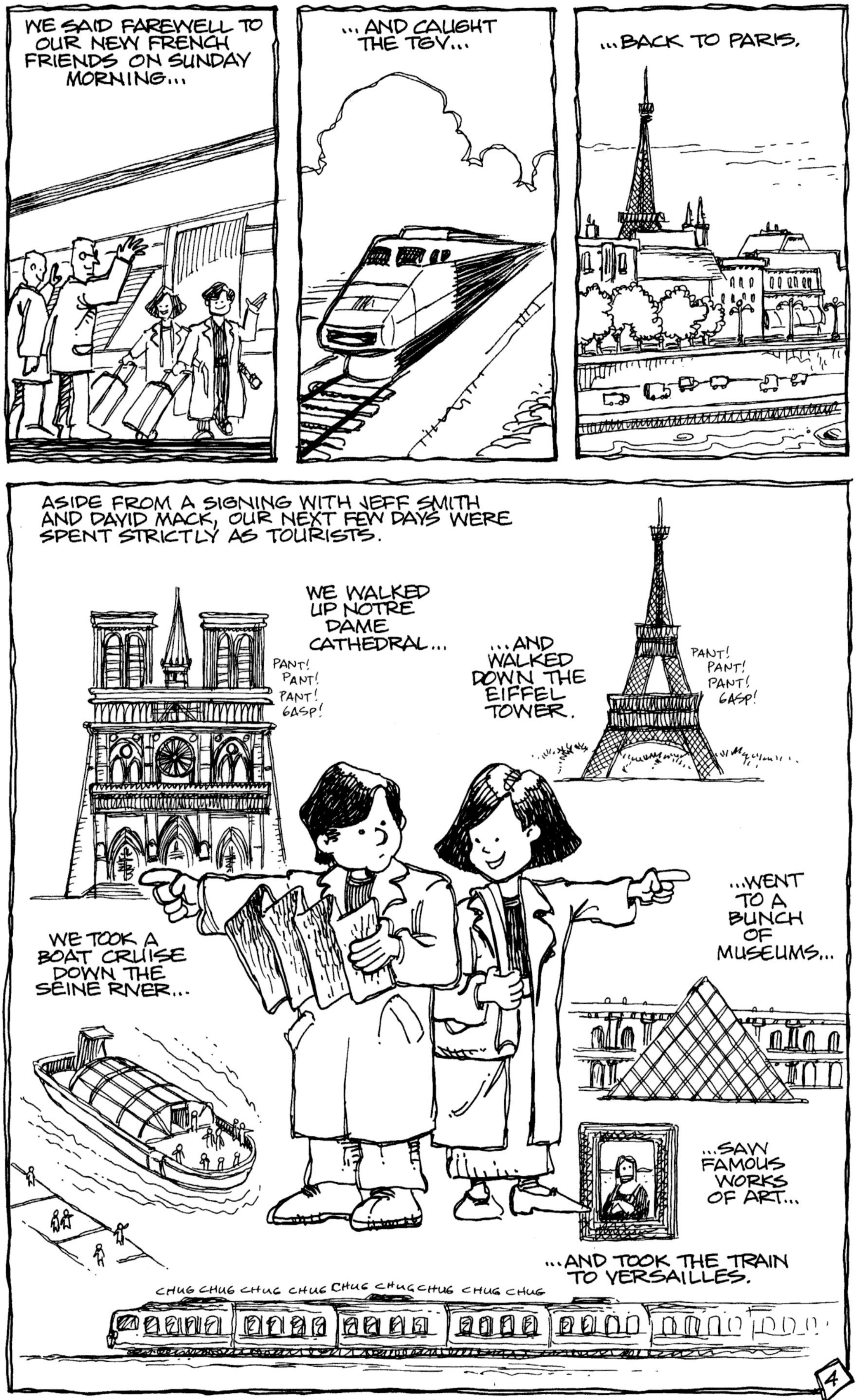
WE SAID FAREWELL TO OUR NEW FRENCH FRIENDS ON SUNDAY MORNING...
...AND CAUGHT THE TGV...
...BACK TO PARIS.
ASIDE FROM A SIGNING WITH JEFF SMITH AND DAVID MACK, OUR NEXT FEW DAYS WERE SPENT STRICTLY AS TOURISTS.
WE WALKED UP NOTRE DAME CATHEDRAL...
PANT! PANT! PANT! GASP!
...AND WALKED DOWN THE EIFFEL TOWER.
PANT! PANT! PANT! GASP!
WE TOOK A BOAT CRUISE DOWN THE SEINE RIVER...
...WENT TO A BUNCH OF MUSEUMS...
...SAW FAMOUS WORKS OF ART...
...AND TOOK THE TRAIN TO VERSAILLES.
CHUG CHUG CHUG CHUG CHUG CHUG CHUG CHUG CHUG
4

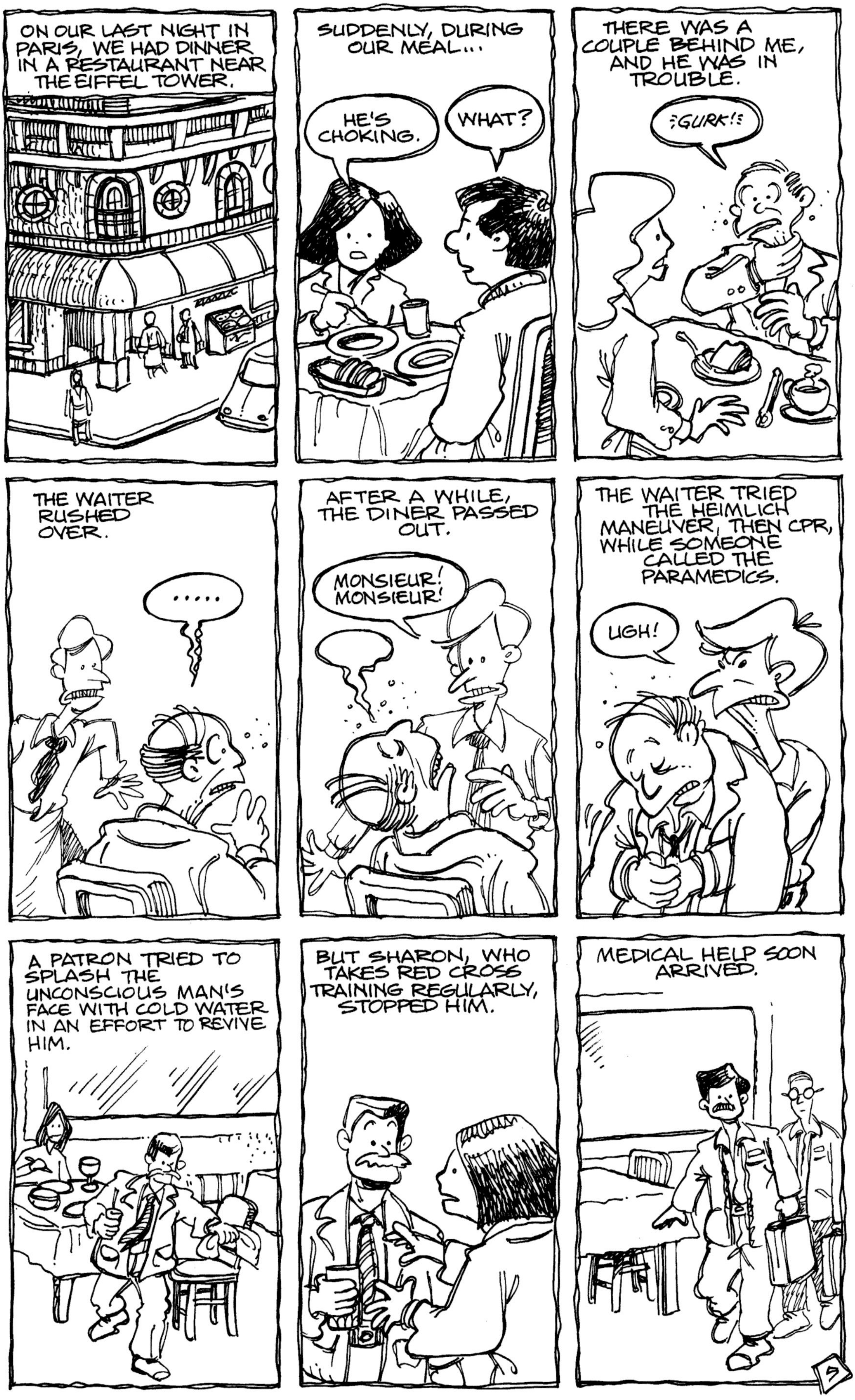
ON OUR LAST NIGHT IN PARIS, WE HAD DINNER IN A RESTAURANT NEAR THE EIFFEL TOWER.
SUDDENLY, DURING OUR MEAL...
HE'S CHOKING.
WHAT?
THERE WAS A COUPLE BEHIND ME, AND HE WAS IN TROUBLE.
GURK!
THE WAITER RUSHED OVER.
.....
AFTER A WHILE, THE DINER PASSED OUT.
MONSIEUR! MONSIEUR!
THE WAITER TRIED THE HEIMLICH MANEUVER, THEN CPR, WHILE SOMEONE CALLED THE PARAMEDICS.
UGH!
A PATRON TRIED TO SPLASH THE UNCONSCIOUS MAN'S FACE WITH COLD WATER IN AN EFFORT TO REVIVE HIM.
BUT SHARON, WHO TAKES RED CROSS TRAINING REGULARLY, STOPPED HIM.
MEDICAL HELP SOON ARRIVED.

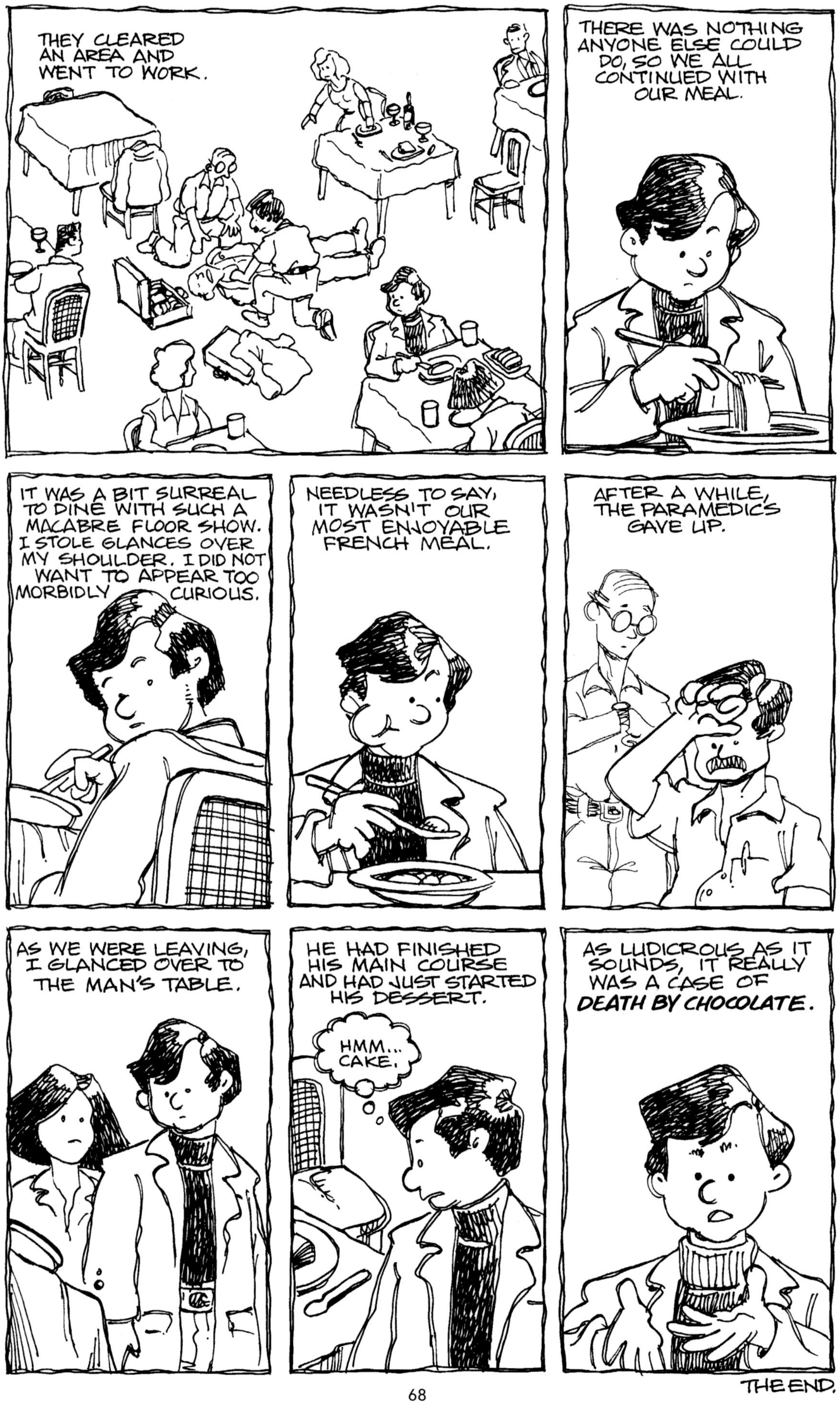
THEY CLEARED AN AREA AND WENT TO WORK.
THERE WAS NOTHING ANYONE ELSE COULD DO, SO WE ALL CONTINUED WITH OUR MEAL.
IT WAS A BIT SURREAL TO DINE WITH SUCH A MACABRE FLOOR SHOW. I STOLE GLANCES OVER MY SHOULDER. I DID NOT WANT TO APPEAR TOO MORBIDLY CURIOUS.
NEEDLESS TO SAY, IT WASN'T OUR MOST ENJOYABLE FRENCH MEAL.
AFTER A WHILE, THE PARAMEDICS GAVE UP.
AS WE WERE LEAVING, I GLANCED OVER TO THE MAN'S TABLE.
HE HAD FINISHED HIS MAIN COURSE AND HAD JUST STARTED HIS DESSERT.
HMM... CAKE.
AS LUDICROUS AS IT SOUNDS, IT REALLY WAS A CASE OF ***DEATH BY CHOCOLATE***.
THE END.

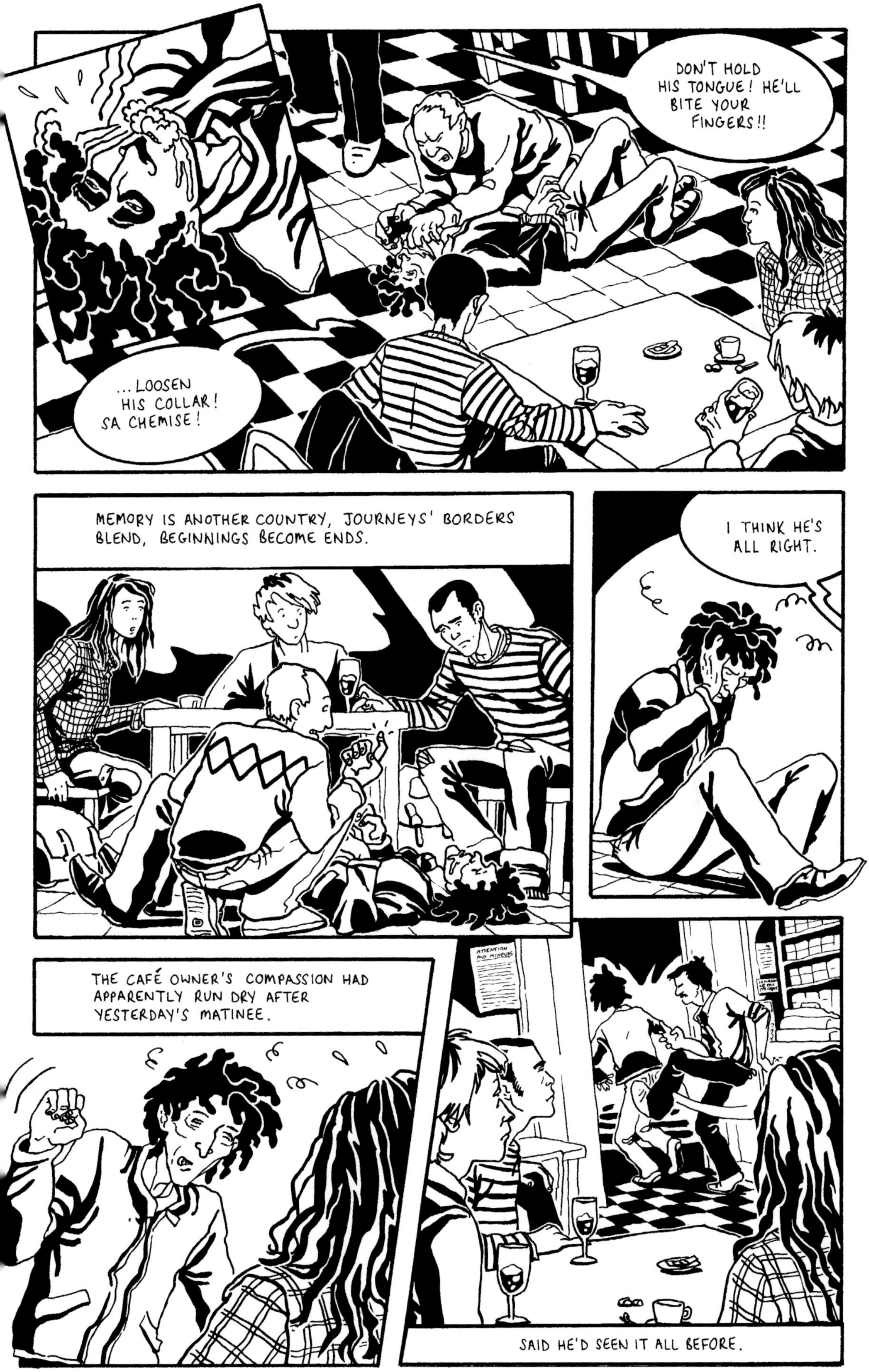
DON'T HOLD HIS TONGUE! HE'LL BITE YOUR FINGERS!!
...LOOSEN HIS COLLAR! SA CHEMISE!
MEMORY IS ANOTHER COUNTRY, JOURNEYS' BORDERS BLEND, BEGINNINGS BECOME ENDS.
I THINK HE'S ALL RIGHT.
THE CAFÉ OWNER'S COMPASSION HAD APPARENTLY RUN DRY AFTER YESTERDAY'S MATINEE.
SAID HE'D SEEN IT ALL BEFORE.

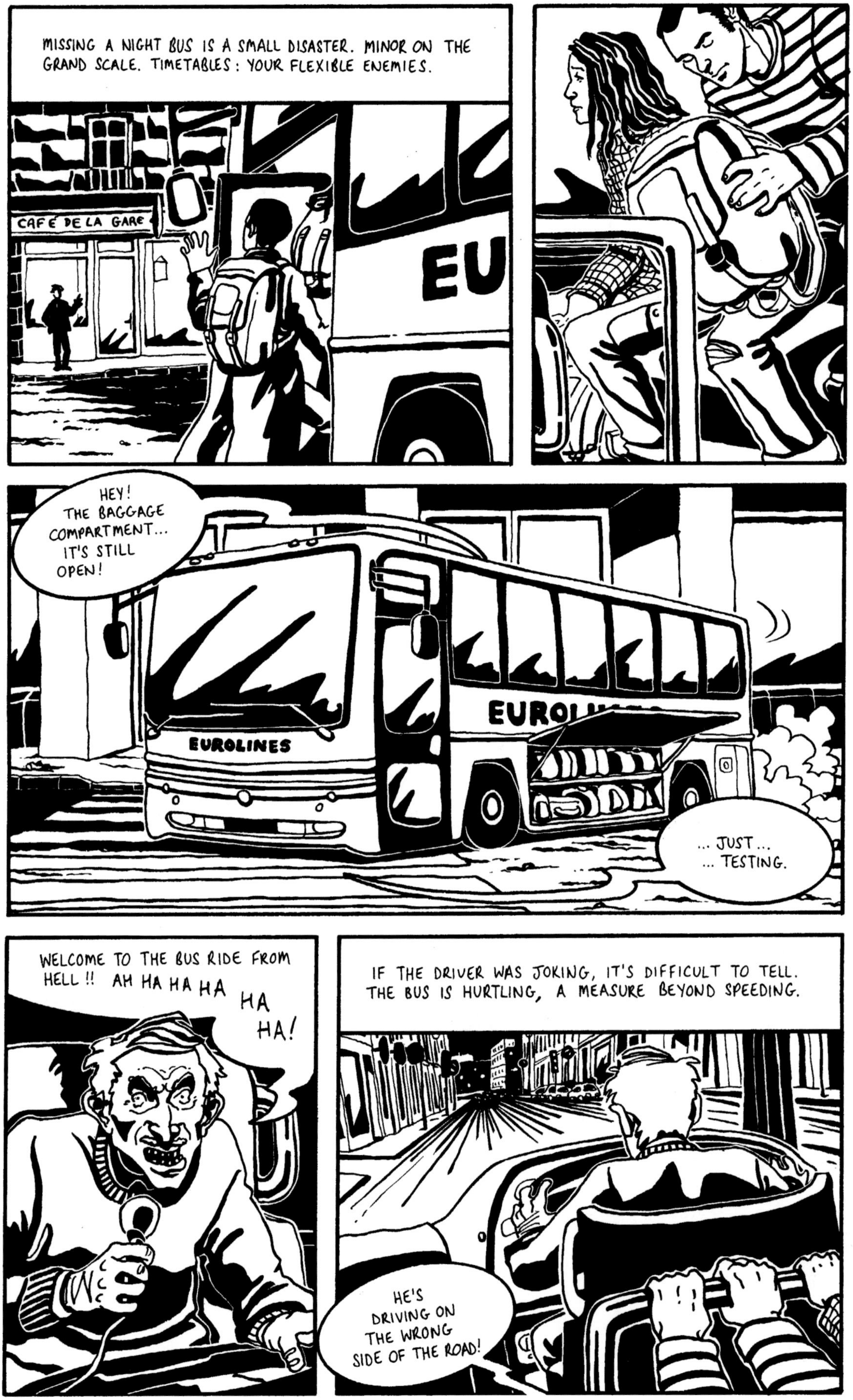
MISSING A NIGHT BUS IS A SMALL DISASTER. MINOR ON THE GRAND SCALE. TIMETABLES: YOUR FLEXIBLE ENEMIES.
CAFÉ DE LA GARE
EU
HEY! THE BAGGAGE COMPARTMENT... IT'S STILL OPEN!
EUROLINES
EURO
... JUST ... ... TESTING.
WELCOME TO THE BUS RIDE FROM HELL !! AH HA HA HA HA HA!
IF THE DRIVER WAS JOKING, IT'S DIFFICULT TO TELL. THE BUS IS HURTLING, A MEASURE BEYOND SPEEDING.
HE'S DRIVING ON THE WRONG SIDE OF THE ROAD!

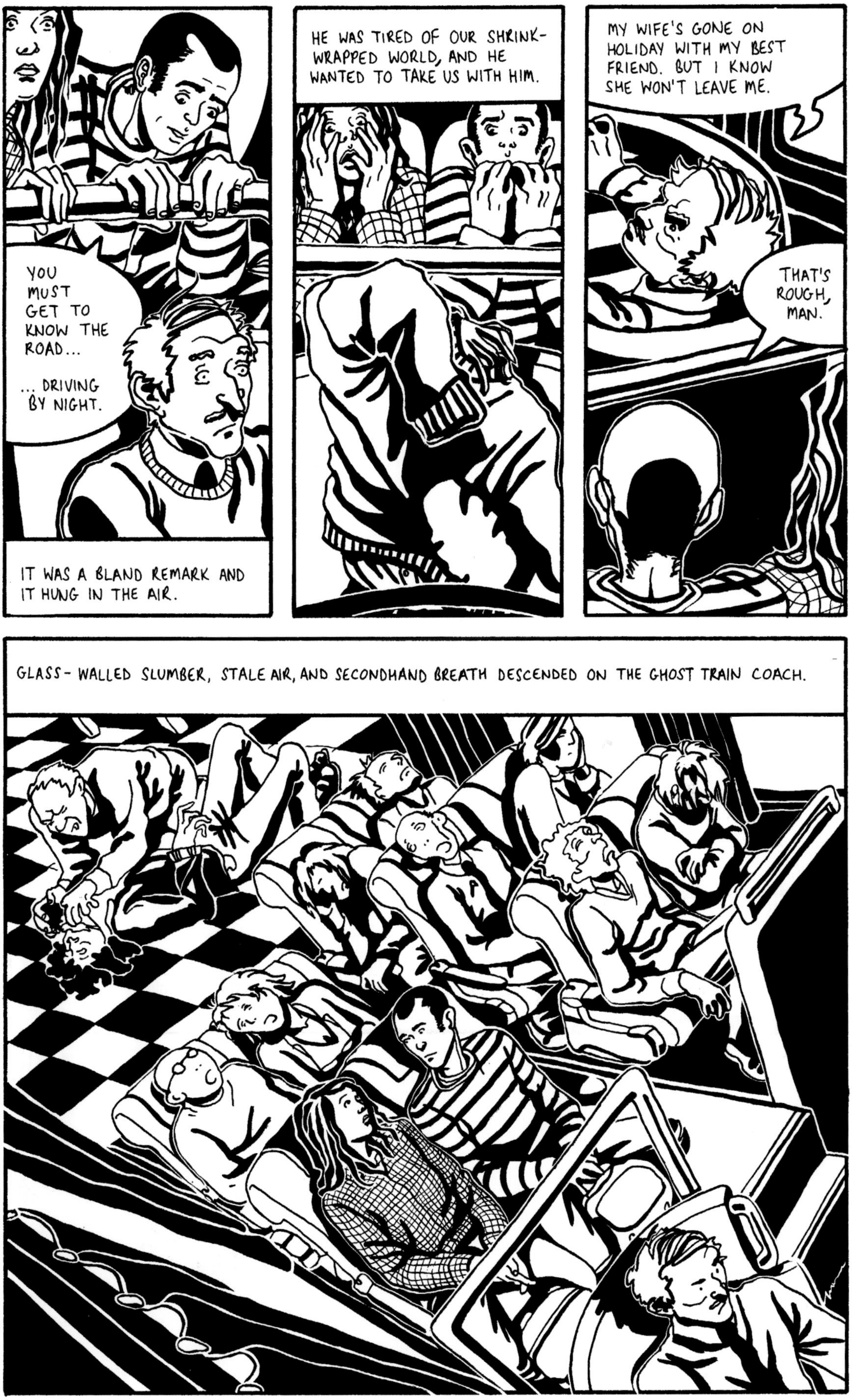
YOU MUST GET TO KNOW THE ROAD...
... DRIVING BY NIGHT.
IT WAS A BLAND REMARK AND IT HUNG IN THE AIR.
HE WAS TIRED OF OUR SHRINK-WRAPPED WORLD, AND HE WANTED TO TAKE US WITH HIM.
MY WIFE'S GONE ON HOLIDAY WITH MY BEST FRIEND. BUT I KNOW SHE WON'T LEAVE ME.
THAT'S ROUGH, MAN.
GLASS-WALLED SLUMBER, STALE AIR, AND SECONDHAND BREATH DESCENDED ON THE GHOST TRAIN COACH.

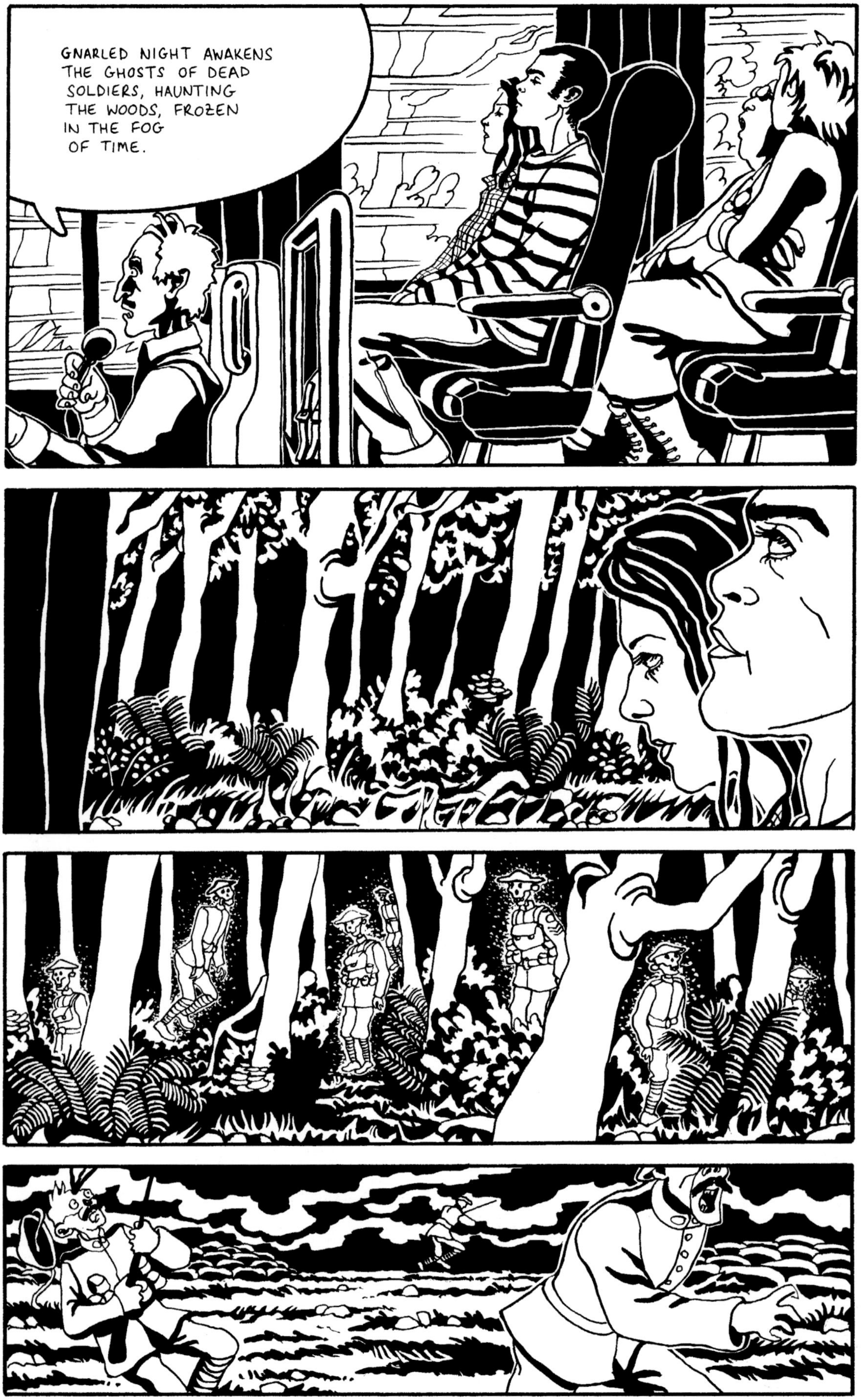
GNARLED NIGHT AWAKENS THE GHOSTS OF DEAD SOLDIERS, HAUNTING THE WOODS, FROZEN IN THE FOG OF TIME.

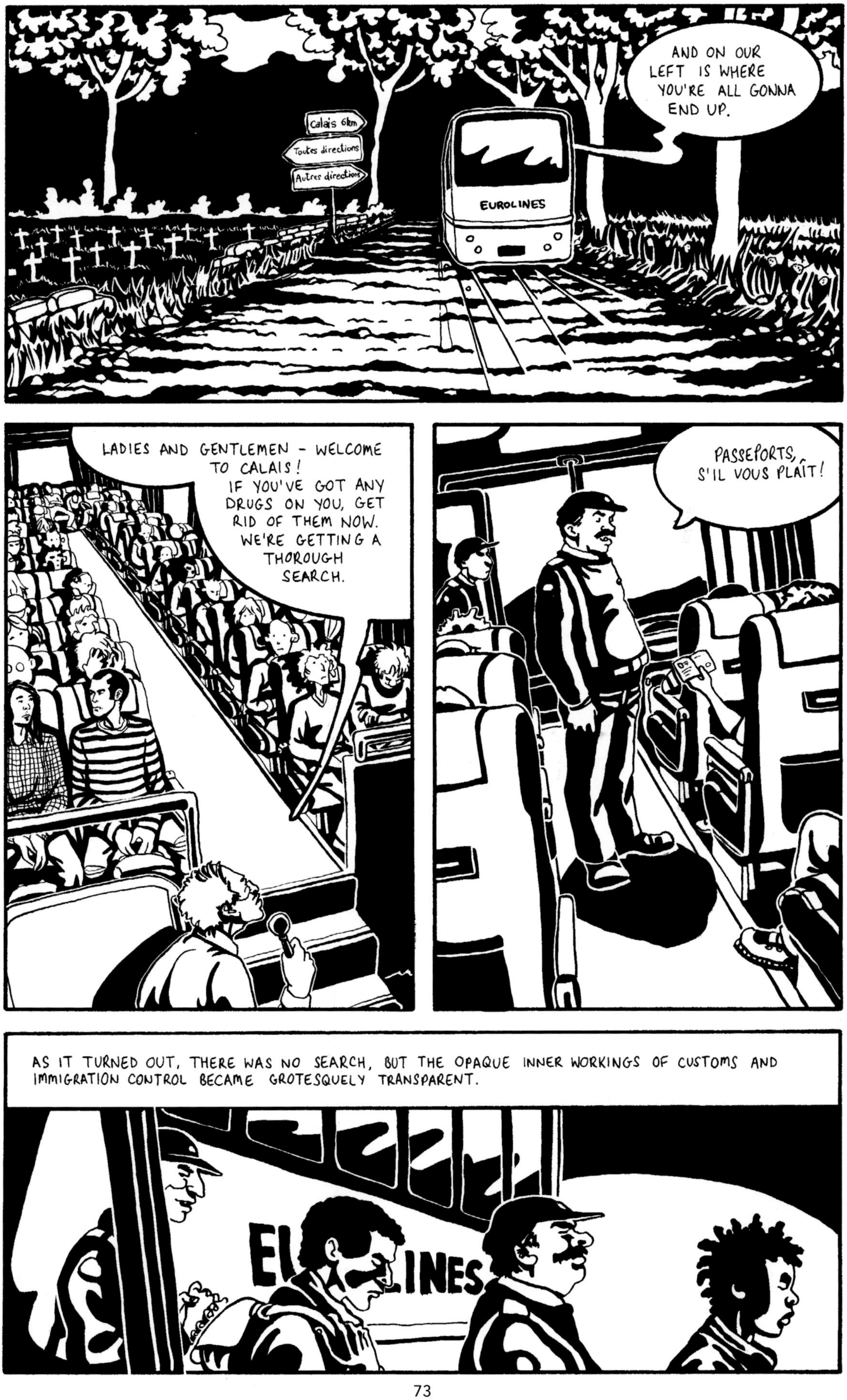
Calais 6km
Toutes directions
Autres directions
EUROLINES
AND ON OUR LEFT IS WHERE YOU'RE ALL GONNA END UP.
LADIES AND GENTLEMEN - WELCOME TO CALAIS! IF YOU'VE GOT ANY DRUGS ON YOU, GET RID OF THEM NOW. WE'RE GETTING A THOROUGH SEARCH.
PASSEPORTS, S'IL VOUS PLAÎT!
AS IT TURNED OUT, THERE WAS NO SEARCH, BUT THE OPAQUE INNER WORKINGS OF CUSTOMS AND IMMIGRATION CONTROL BECAME GROTESQUELY TRANSPARENT.

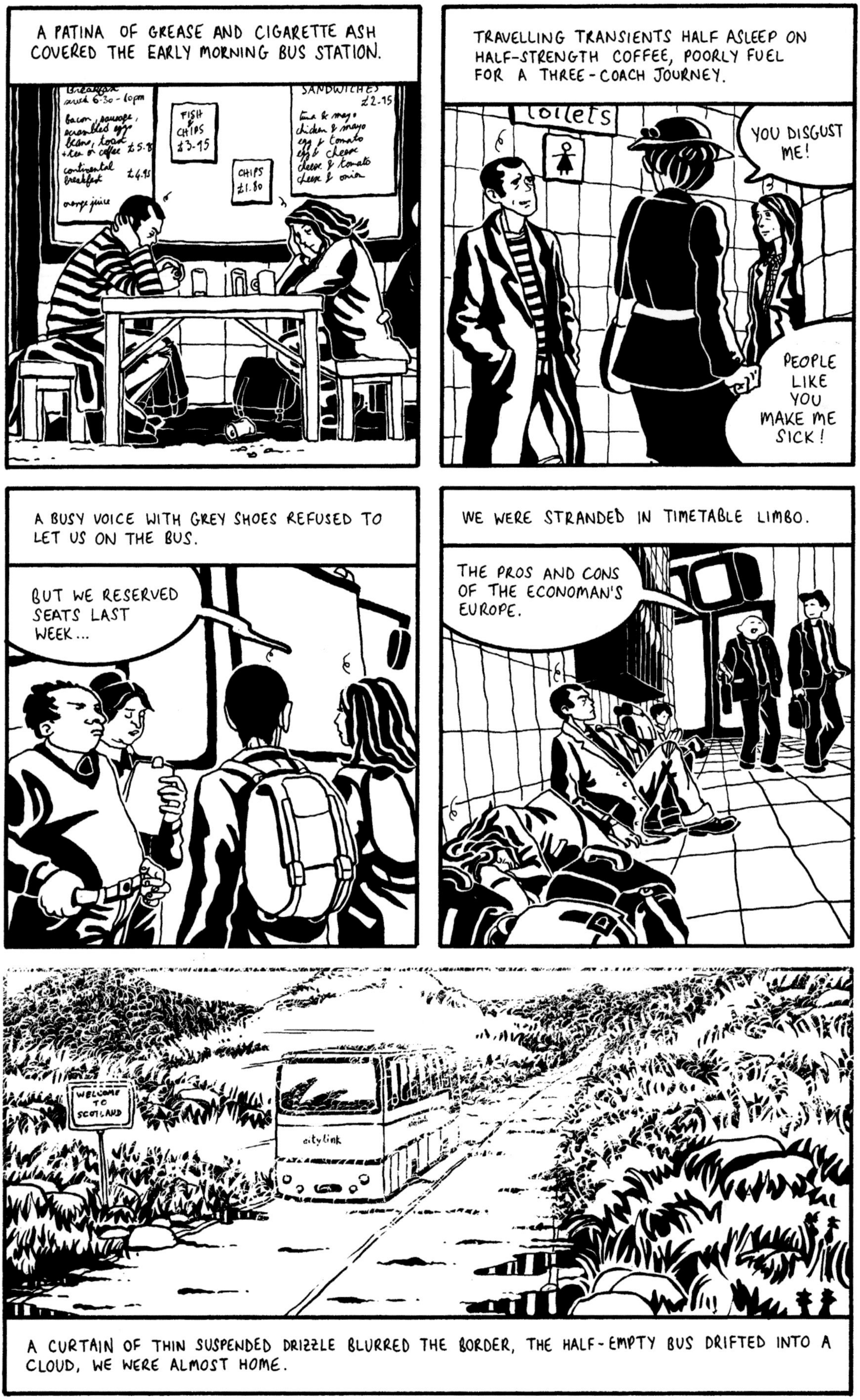
A PATINA OF GREASE AND CIGARETTE ASH COVERED THE EARLY MORNING BUS STATION.
FISH & CHIPS £3-95
CHIPS £1.80
TRAVELLING TRANSIENTS HALF ASLEEP ON HALF-STRENGTH COFFEE, POORLY FUEL FOR A THREE-COACH JOURNEY.
TOILETS
YOU DISGUST ME!
PEOPLE LIKE YOU MAKE ME SICK!
A BUSY VOICE WITH GREY SHOES REFUSED TO LET US ON THE BUS.
BUT WE RESERVED SEATS LAST WEEK...
WE WERE STRANDED IN TIMETABLE LIMBO.
THE PROS AND CONS OF THE ECONOMAN'S EUROPE.
WELCOME TO SCOTLAND
citylink
A CURTAIN OF THIN SUSPENDED DRIZZLE BLURRED THE BORDER, THE HALF-EMPTY BUS DRIFTED INTO A CLOUD, WE WERE ALMOST HOME.

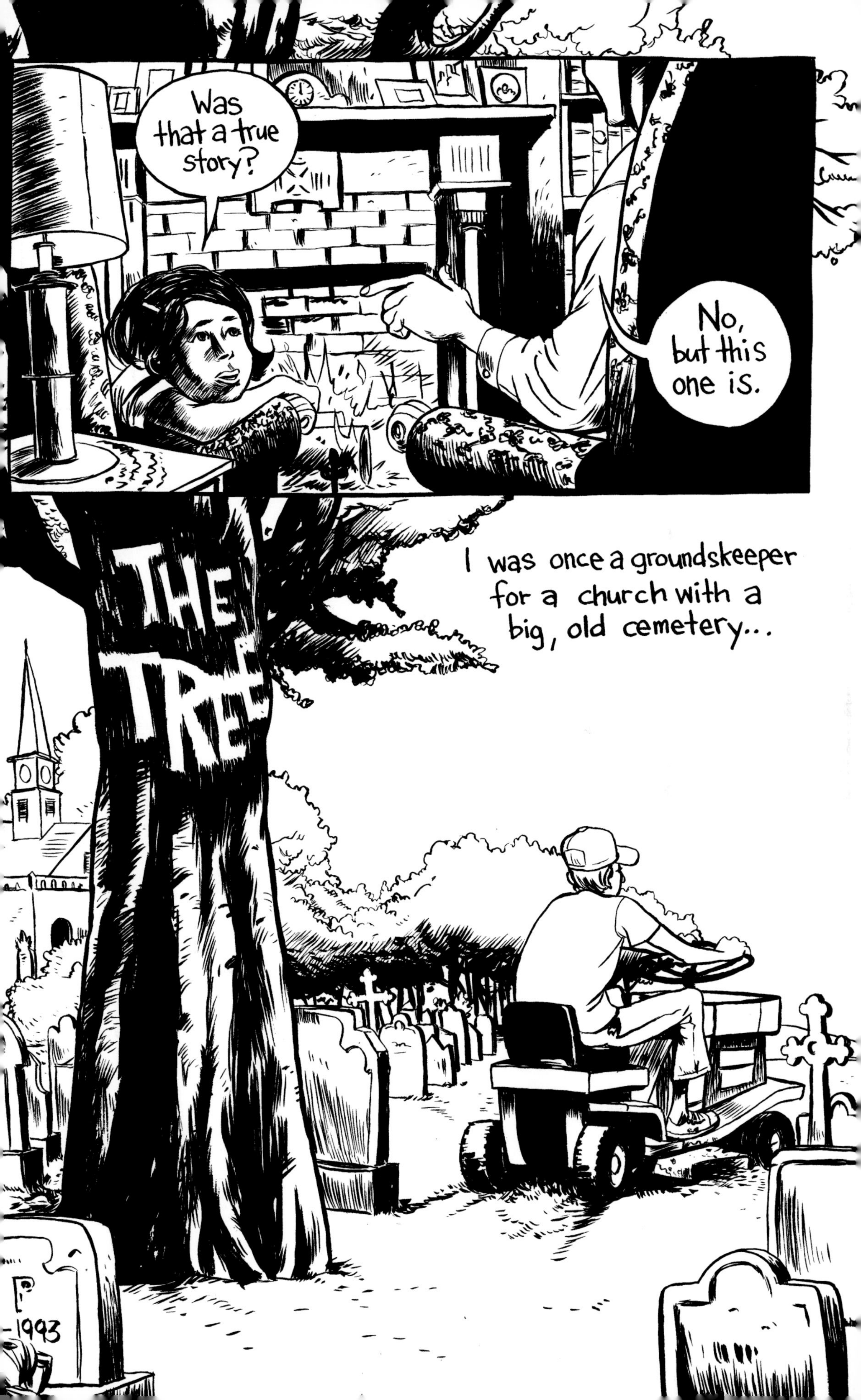
Was that a true story?
No, but this one is.
THE TREE
I was once a groundskeeper for a church with a big, old cemetery...
1993

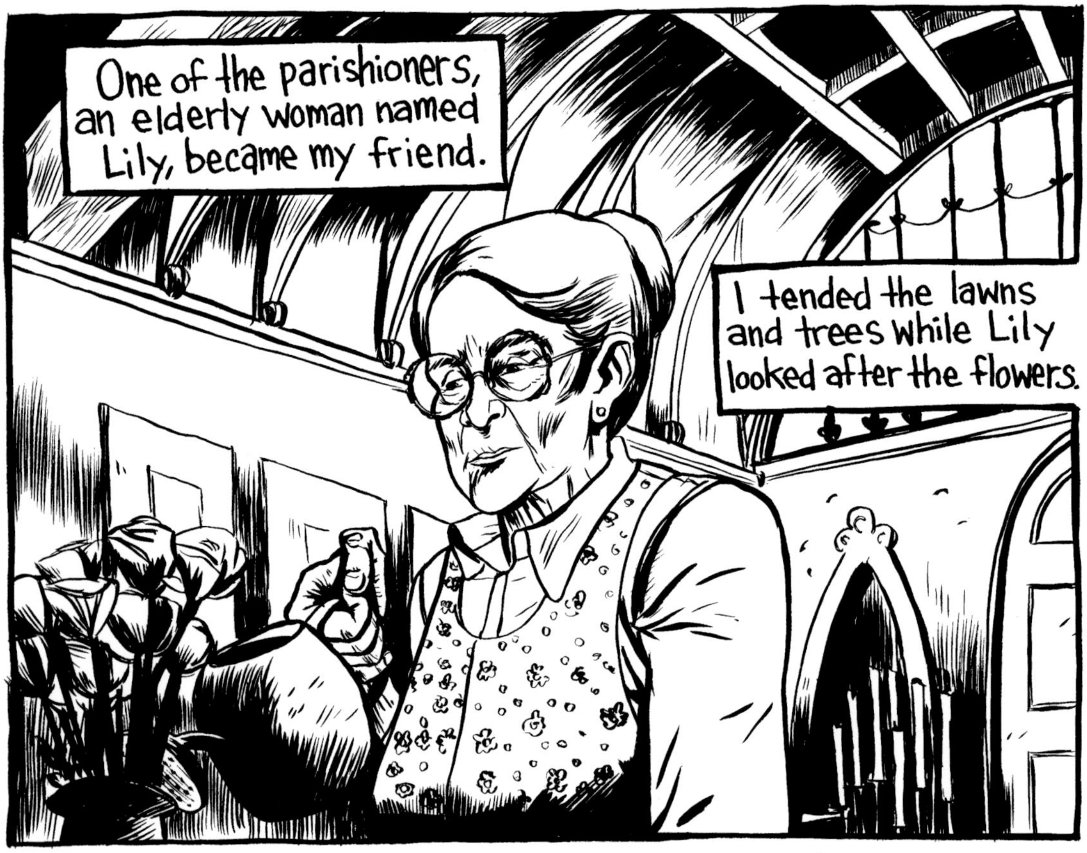
One of the parishioners, an elderly woman named Lily, became my friend.
I tended the lawns and trees while Lily looked after the flowers.

She had always lived in the parish. Her parents were buried in that cemetery.

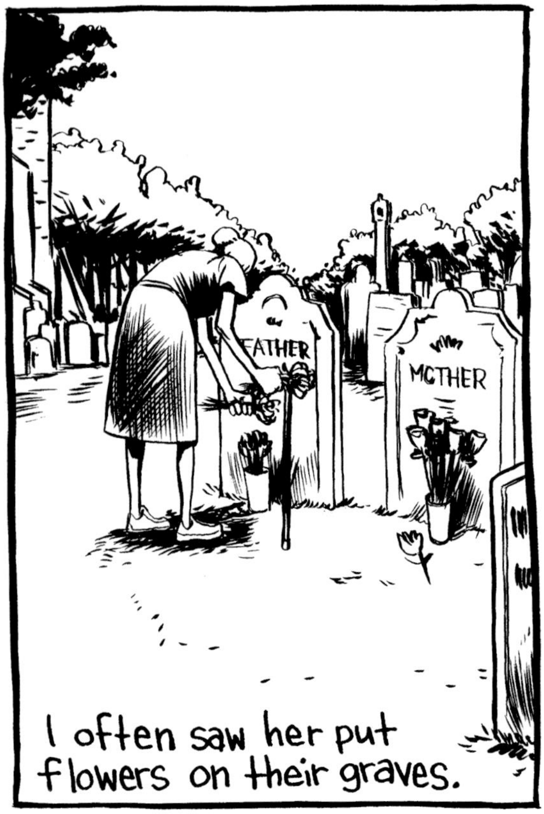
FATHER
MOTHER
I often saw her put flowers on their graves.

One day Lily pulled me aside...

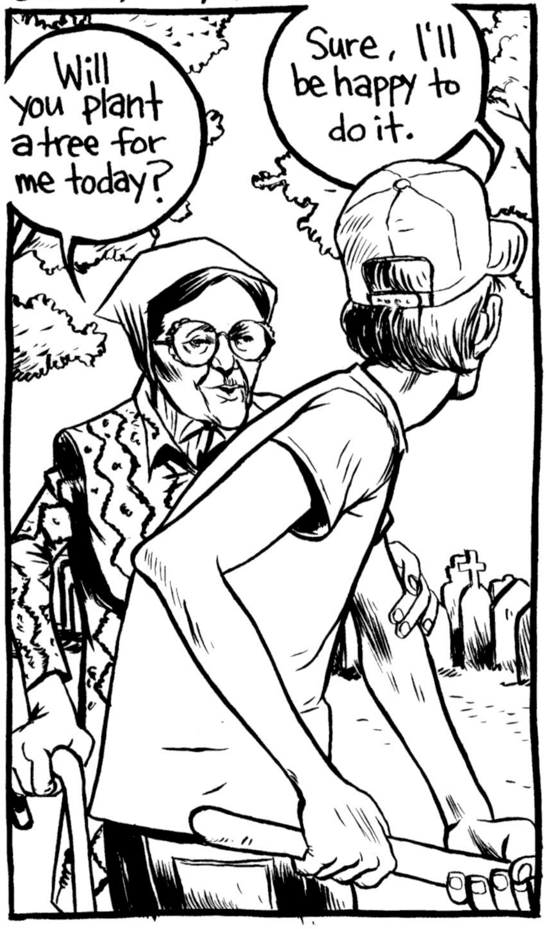
Will you plant a tree for me today?
Sure, I'll be happy to do it.

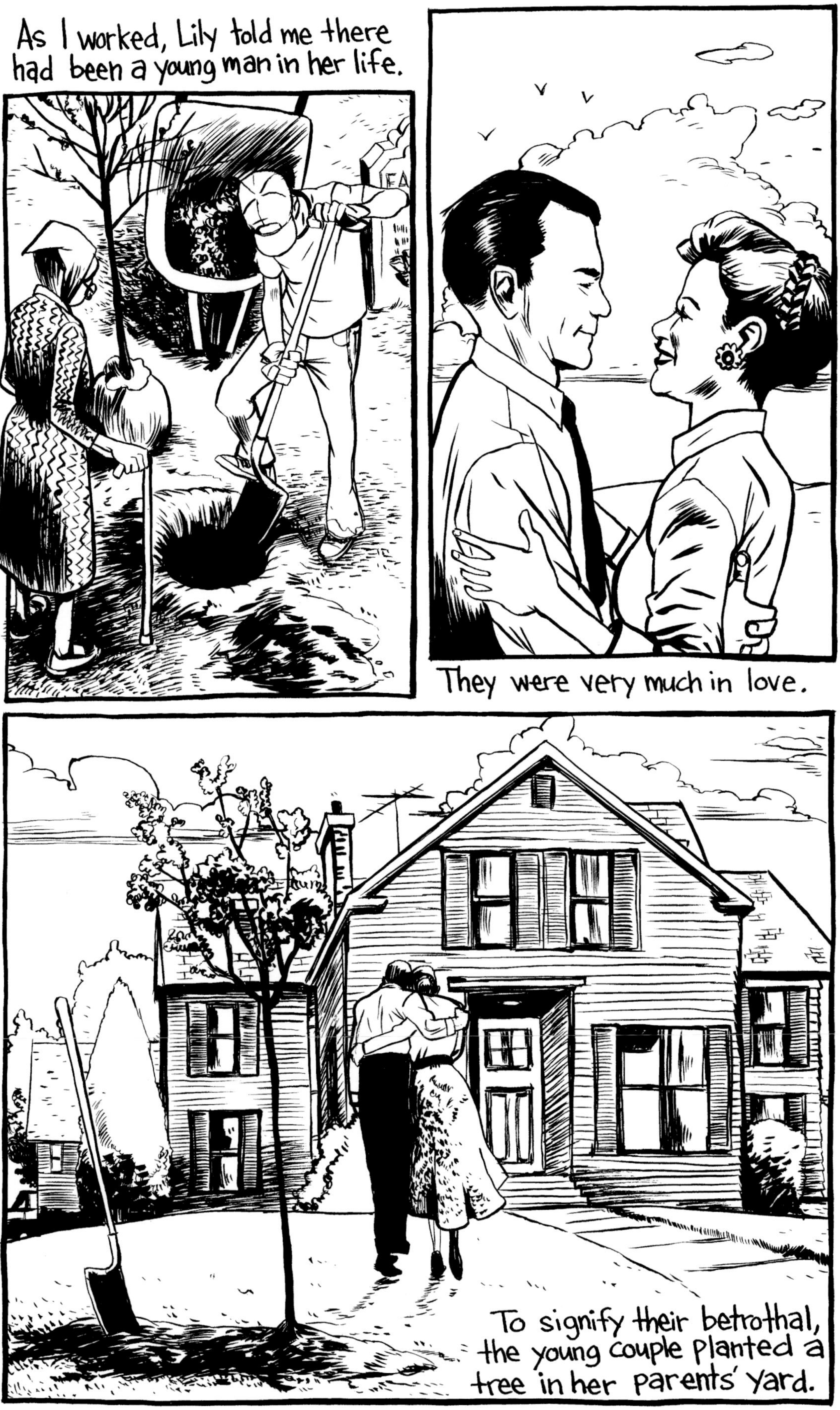
As I worked, Lily told me there had been a young man in her life.
They were very much in love.
To signify their betrothal, the young couple planted a tree in her parents' yard.

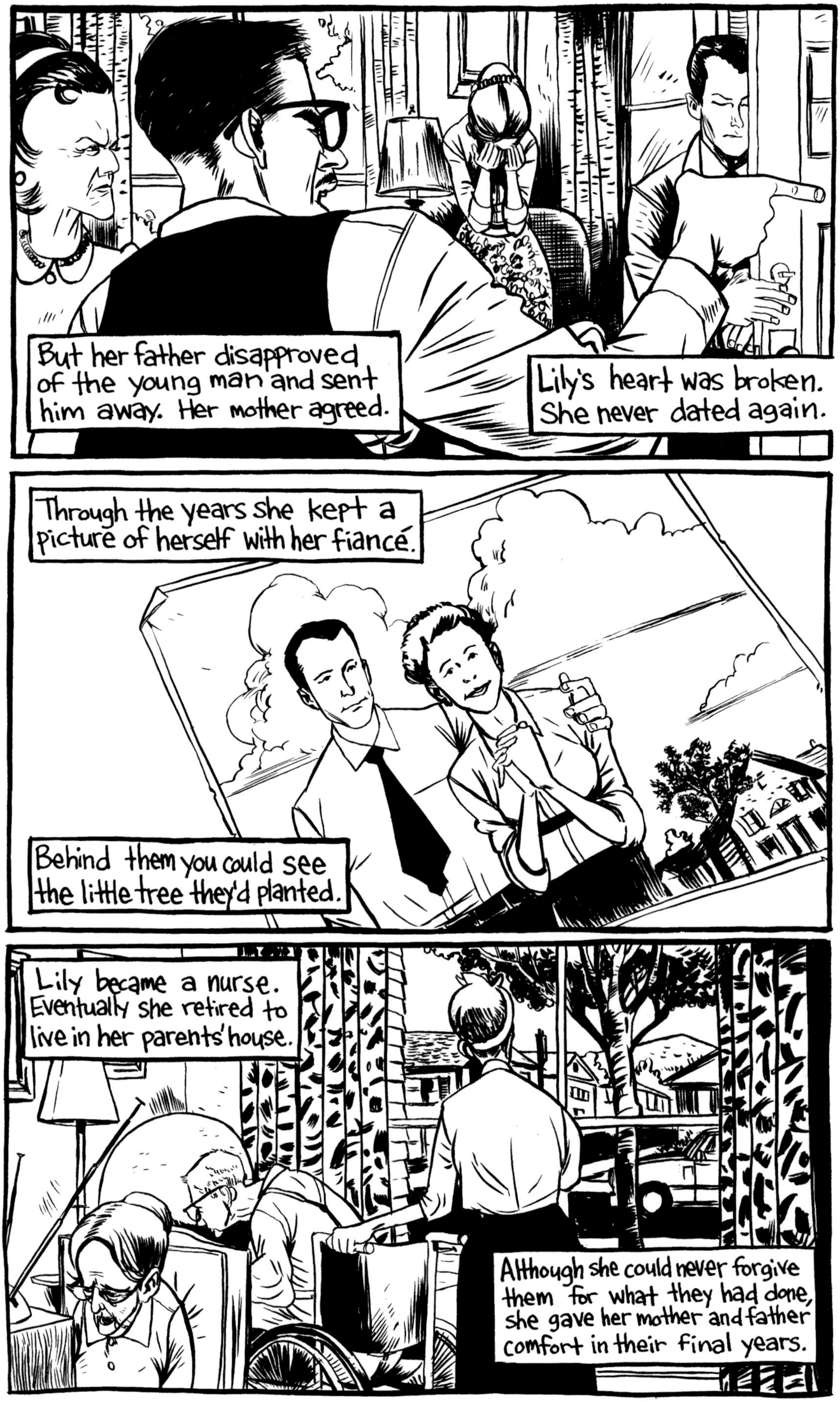
But her father disapproved of the young man and sent him away. Her mother agreed.
Lily's heart was broken. She never dated again.
Through the years she kept a picture of herself with her fiancé.
Behind them you could see the little tree they'd planted.
Lily became a nurse. Eventually she retired to live in her parents' house.
Although she could never forgive them for what they had done, she gave her mother and father comfort in their final years.

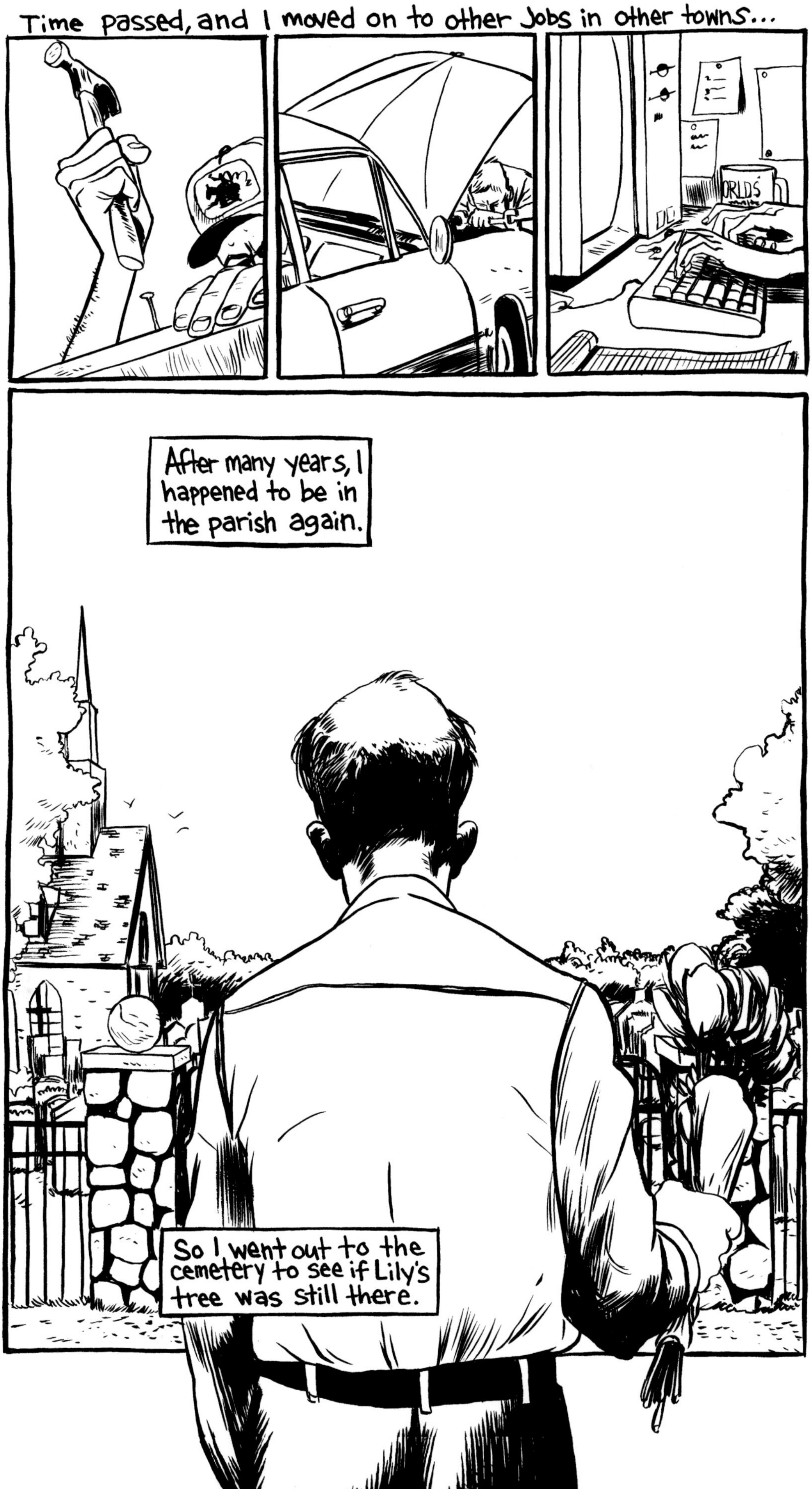
Time passed, and I moved on to other Jobs in other towns...
After many years, I happened to be in the parish again.
So I went out to the cemetery to see if Lily's tree was still there.

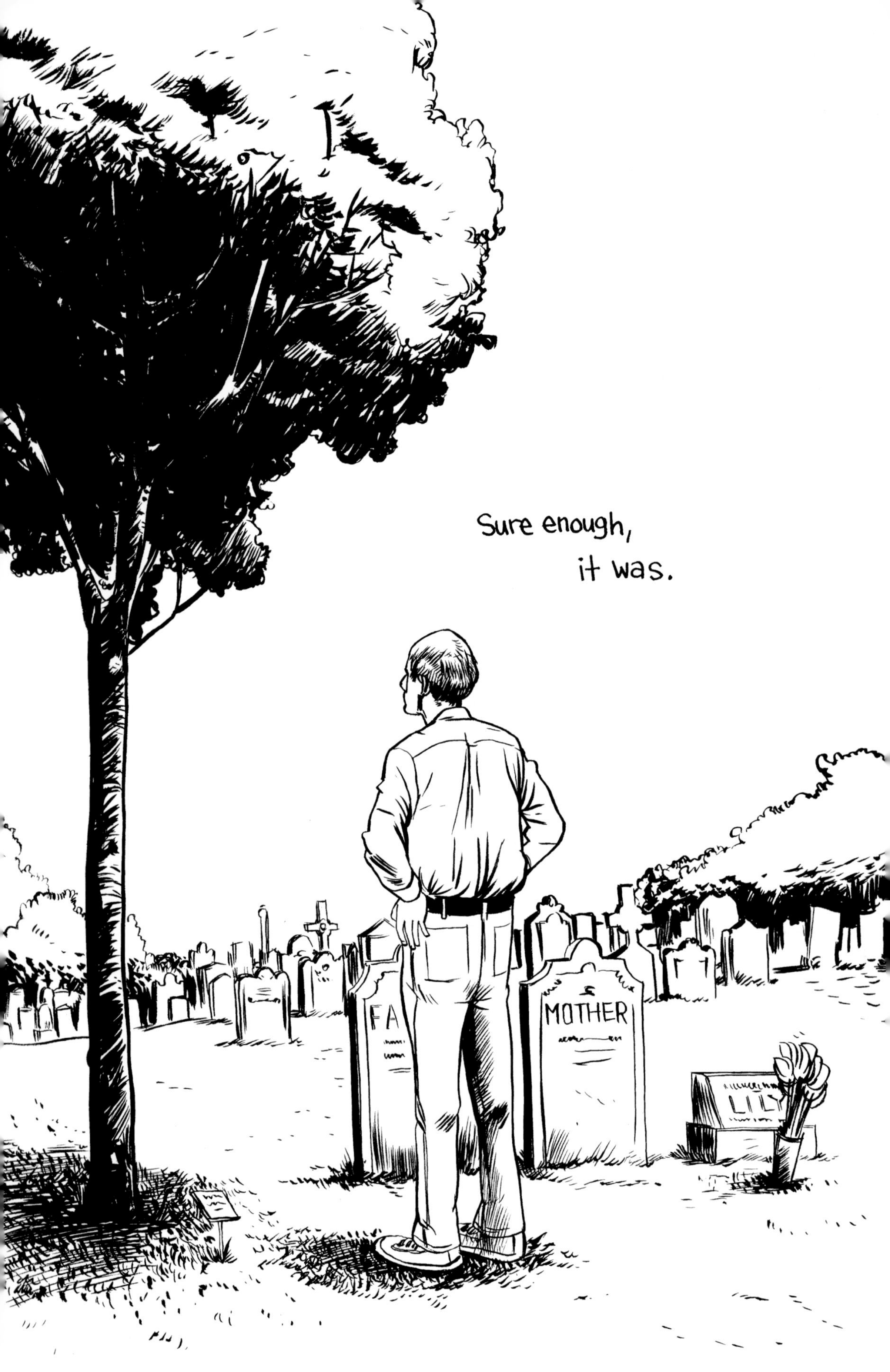
Sure enough,
it was.
MOTHER

HE
GETS
UP.

HE STUMBLES
INTO ROUTINES.

HE BEGINS
TO PANIC.

SIT DOWN.
SIT DOWN.

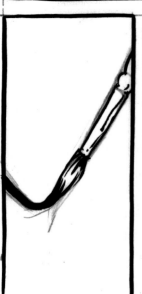

WHERE DOES
HE START?
WHY DOES
HE START?

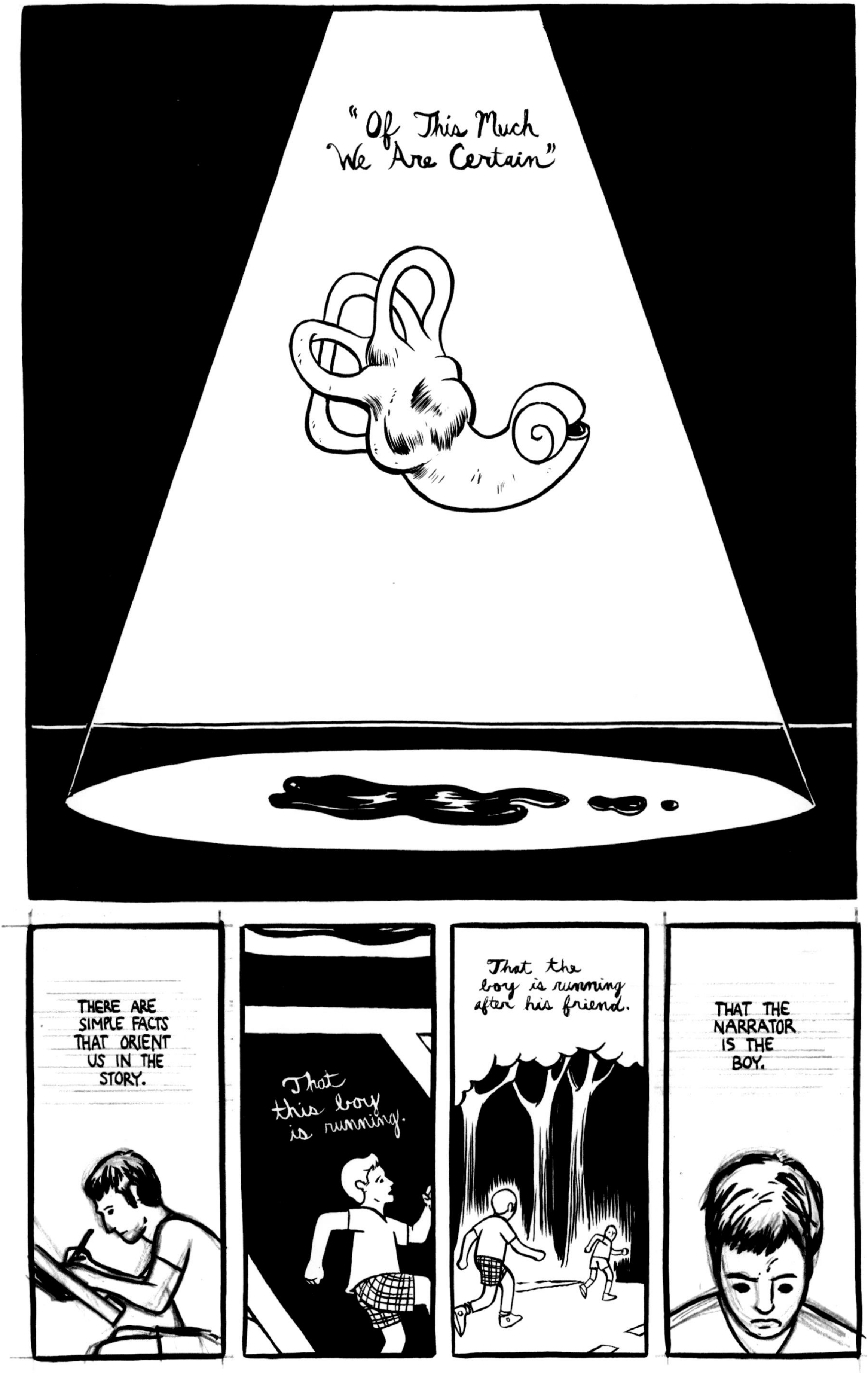
"Of This Much We Are Certain"
THERE ARE SIMPLE FACTS THAT ORIENT US IN THE STORY.
That this boy is running.
That the boy is running after his friend.
THAT THE NARRATOR IS THE BOY.

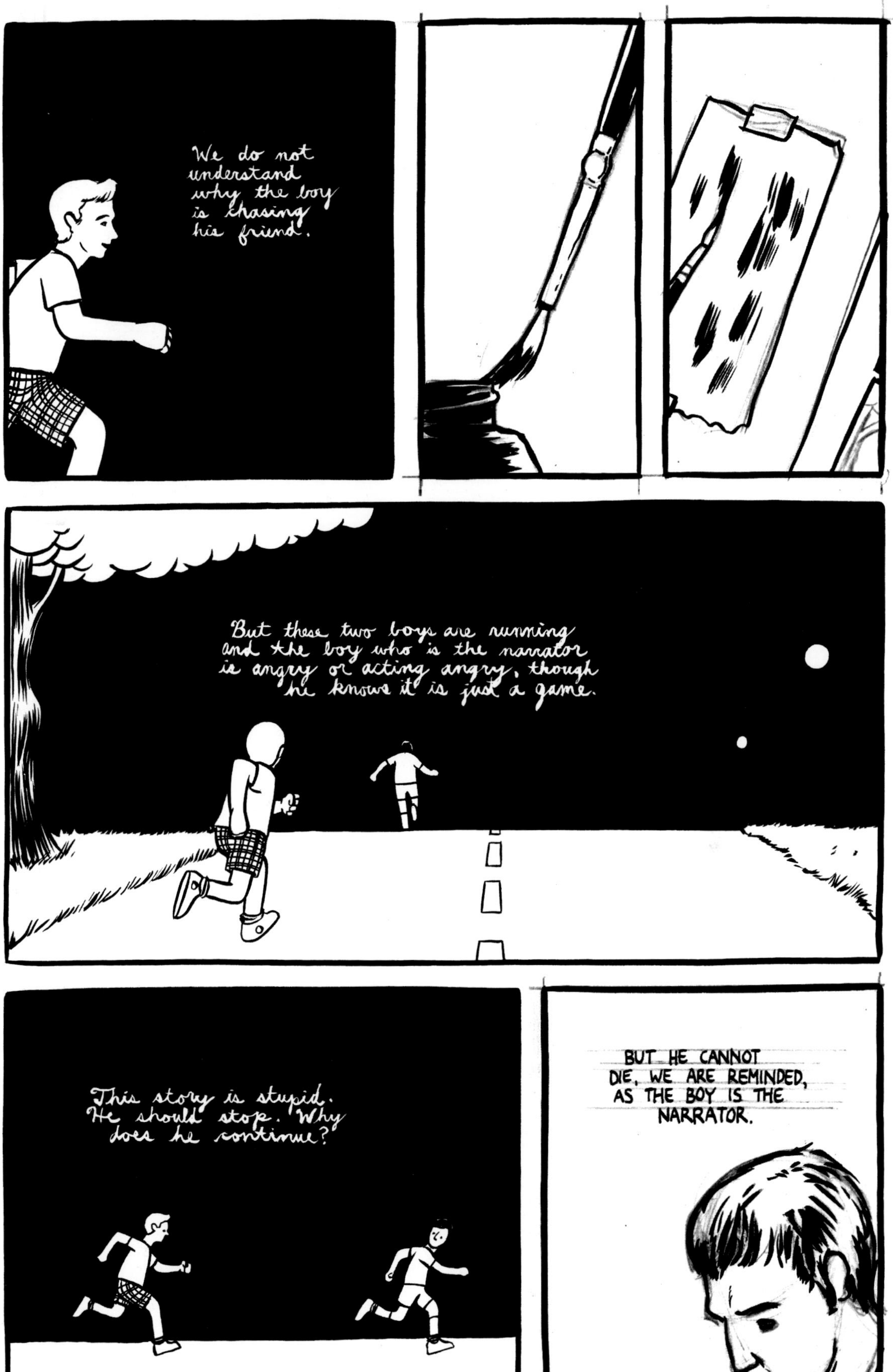
We do not understand why the boy is chasing his friend.
But these two boys are running and the boy who is the narrator is angry or acting angry, though he knows it is just a game.
This story is stupid. He should stop. Why does he continue?
BUT HE CANNOT DIE, WE ARE REMINDED, AS THE BOY IS THE NARRATOR.

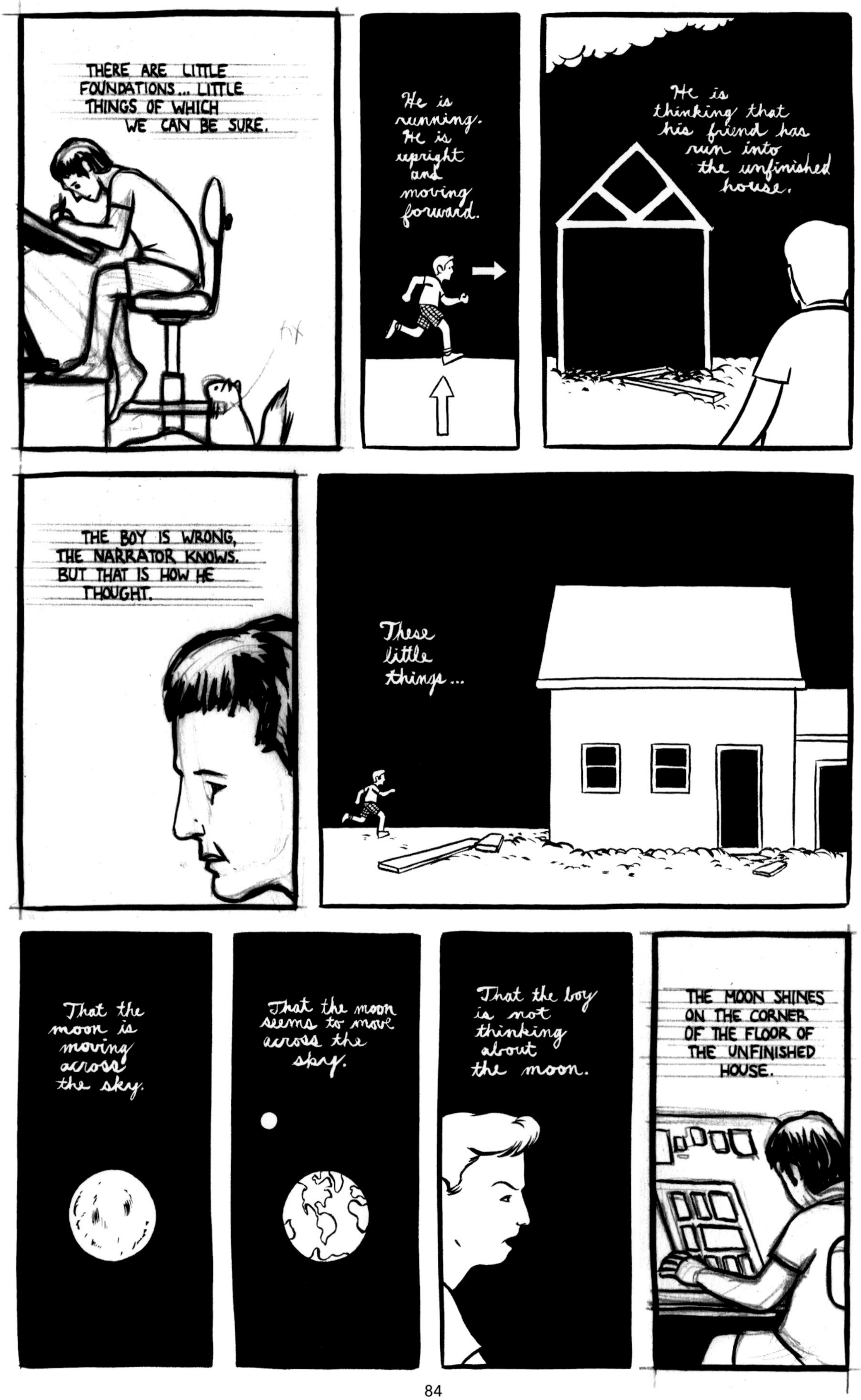
THERE ARE LITTLE FOUNDATIONS... LITTLE THINGS OF WHICH WE CAN BE SURE.
He is running. He is upright and moving forward.
He is thinking that his friend has run into the unfinished house.
THE BOY IS WRONG, THE NARRATOR KNOWS. BUT THAT IS HOW HE THOUGHT.
These little things...
That the moon is moving across the sky.
That the moon seems to move across the sky.
That the boy is not thinking about the moon.
THE MOON SHINES ON THE CORNER OF THE FLOOR OF THE UNFINISHED HOUSE.

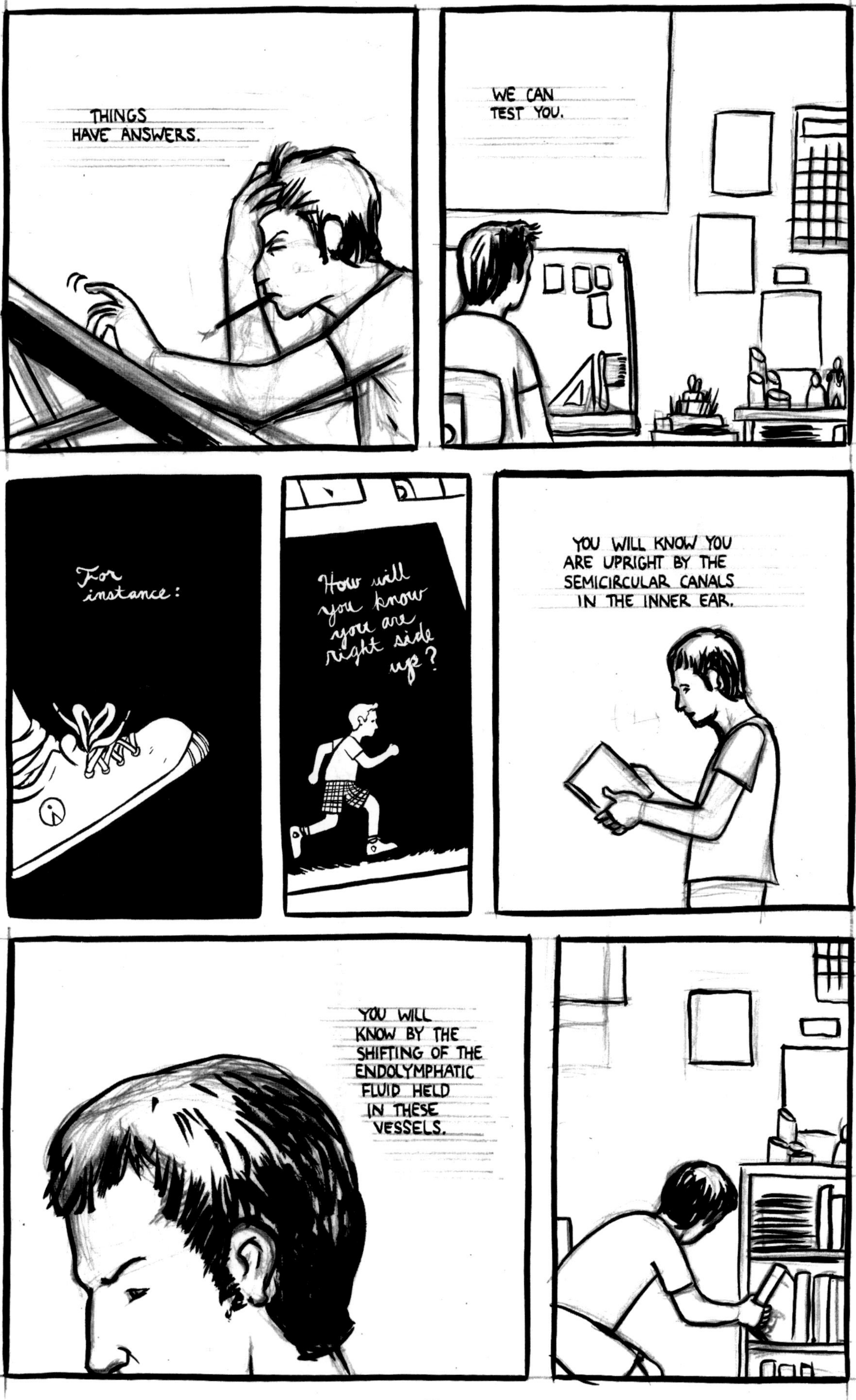
THINGS HAVE ANSWERS.
WE CAN TEST YOU.
For instance:
How will you know you are right side up?
YOU WILL KNOW YOU ARE UPRIGHT BY THE SEMICIRCULAR CANALS IN THE INNER EAR.
YOU WILL KNOW BY THE SHIFTING OF THE ENDOLYMPHATIC FLUID HELD IN THESE VESSELS.

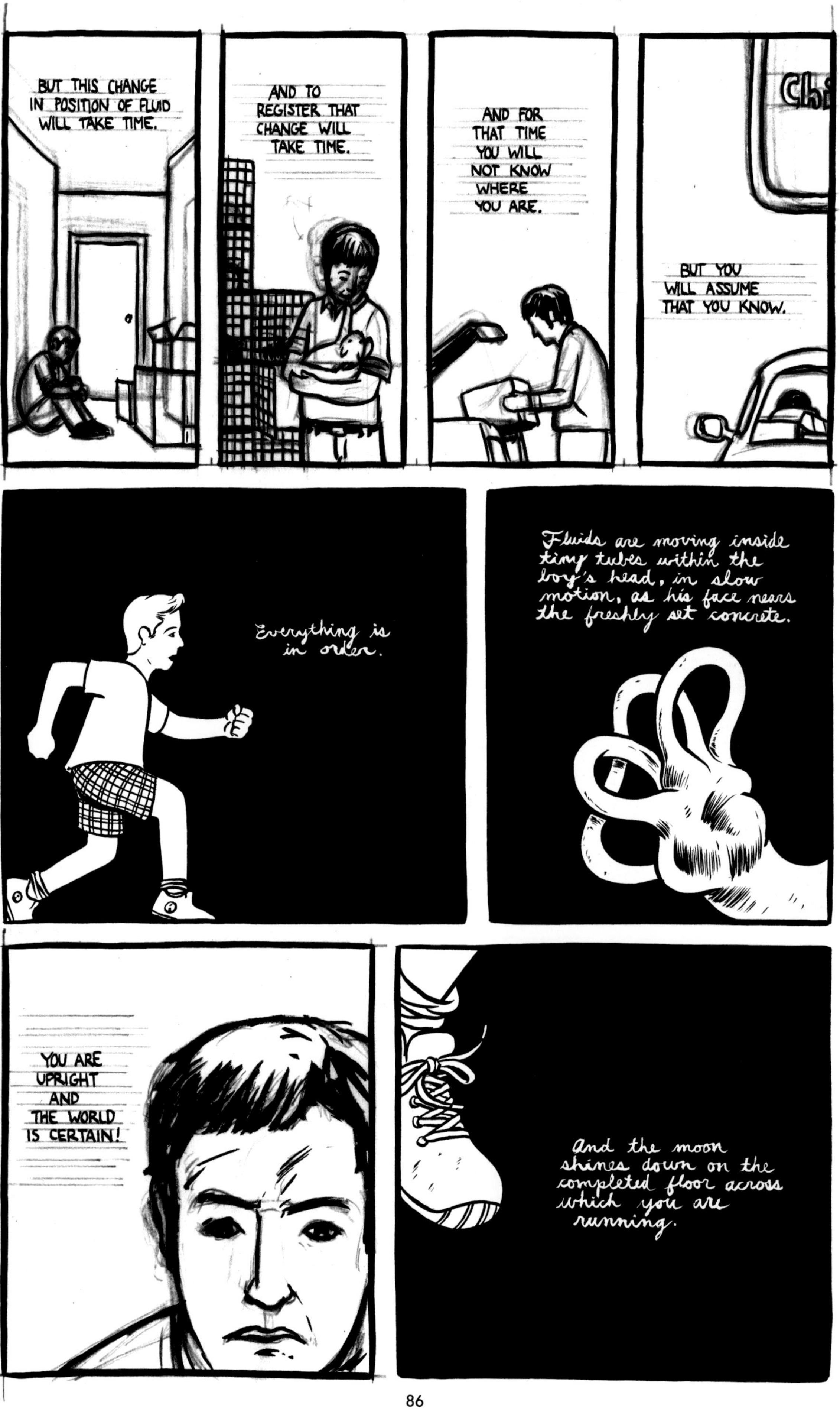
BUT THIS CHANGE IN POSITION OF FLUID WILL TAKE TIME.
AND TO REGISTER THAT CHANGE WILL TAKE TIME.
AND FOR THAT TIME YOU WILL NOT KNOW WHERE YOU ARE.
BUT YOU WILL ASSUME THAT YOU KNOW.
Everything is in order.
Fluids are moving inside tiny tubes within the boy's head, in slow motion, as his face nears the freshly set concrete.
YOU ARE UPRIGHT AND THE WORLD IS CERTAIN!
And the moon shines down on the completed floor across which you are running.

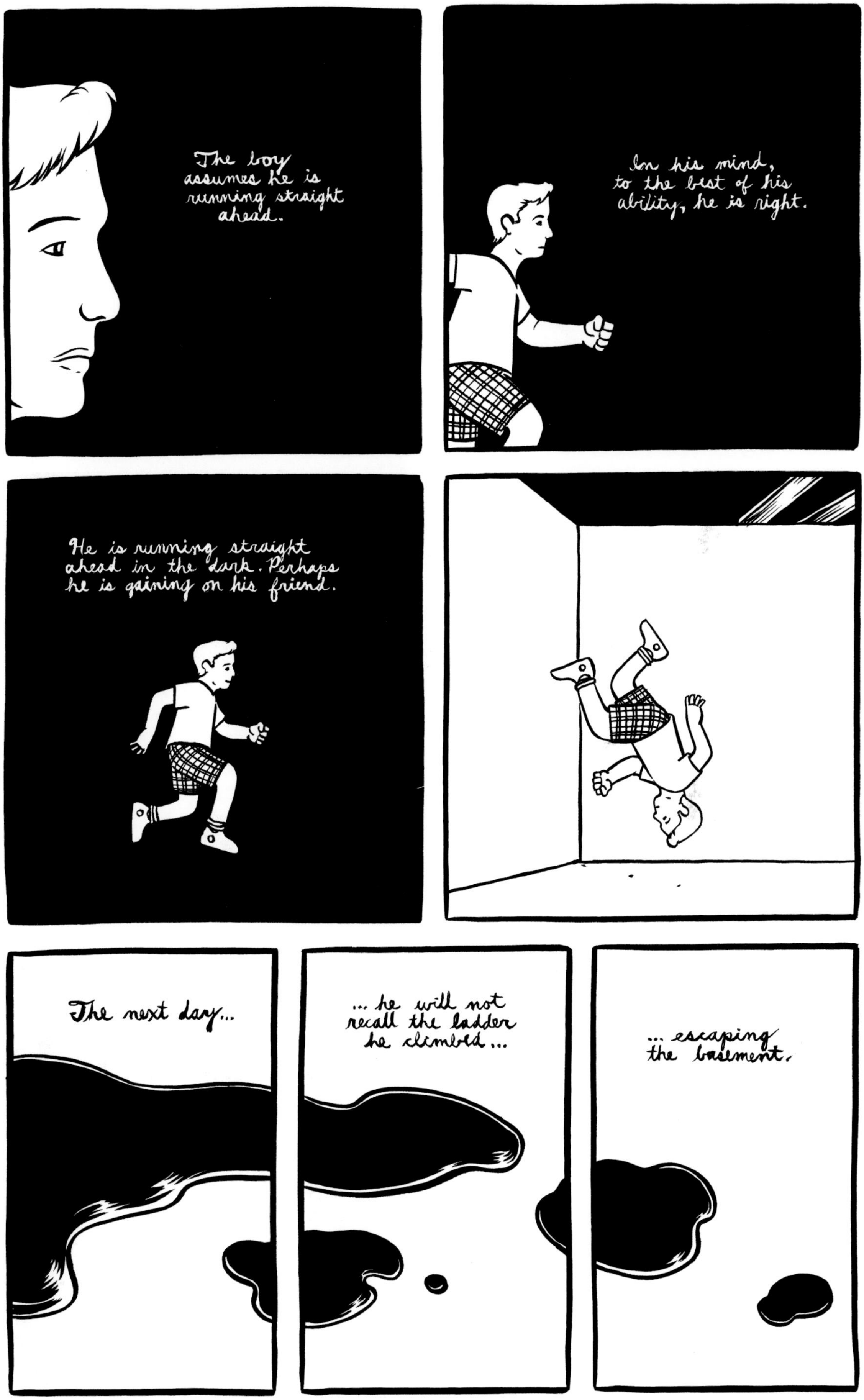
The boy assumes he is running straight ahead.
In his mind, to the best of his ability, he is right.
He is running straight ahead in the dark. Perhaps he is gaining on his friend.
The next day...
... he will not recall the ladder he climbed...
... escaping the basement.

The boy becomes older and the moon moves across the sky.

and the house is built up and the people move in.

and dinners are cooked and the boy goes to college.

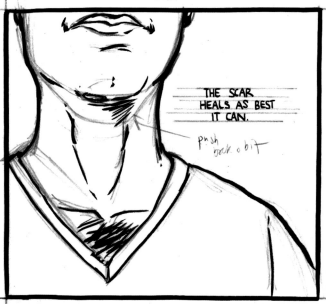

THE SCAR HEALS AS BEST IT CAN.

push back a bit

AND EVERYONE BECOMES MORE SURE.

AND EVERYONE RUNS SMOOTHLY...

...ACROSS THE FINISHED FLOOR AT NIGHT.

AFTERWORD

It was Will Eisner, the grand master of sequential art, who noted that comics came of age with the advent of the undergrounds and their cartoonists' insistence on telling stories from real life. It was at that point, says Will, that the medium made the quantum jump beyond its origins as pulp entertainment and into the heady realm of literature. Not surprisingly, Will himself was a pioneer of first-person narrative in comics, albeit in a fictional context; but it remained to those comix artists of the sixties to lend an autobiographical voice to the medium, for the first time establishing close contact between creator and reader.

There is something about the personal voice that is immediately compelling, and not so much because truth often is stranger than fiction. Truth, after all, is highly selective at the pen of the writer. Rather, it's the confidences shared and the intimacy of connection that invite the reader's involvement. It's an intimacy, a personal touch, even more pronounced in the case of black-and-white comics, wherein the reader directly feels the physicality of the artist's hand across the page. Inking, as Frank Miller has said on more than one occasion—and evidenced at every turn in *Sin City*—is very sexy!

The cartoonists in this volume are storytellers, by definition. For many, however, this was their first, and courageous, leap into telling real-life stories. And the stories run the gamut: from humorous anecdotes to poignant recollections to philosophical ruminations on life. My thanks go to each of the cartoonists herein, especially to those whom I alternately cajoled or browbeat for their participation, for it is no easy matter to bare one's soul in print.

Thanks are also due to Paul Hornschemeier for his elegant design work and to Katie Moody for her invaluable last-minute editorial assistance —not to mention Mike Richardson for continuing to allow me to work on more personal, less strictly commercial projects.

In the time it took for *AutobioGraphix* to go from production to print, reality intruded in my own life. Eric Lindquist, my boyfriend of fourteen months and a day, died suddenly in his home on July 10, 2003, at the too-young age of forty-five. I was the one to find him, and that tragic real-life story will haunt me forever. I had talked several times with him about this project, and he took great delight in my excitement as the anthology began to take shape. I regret that Eric did not live long enough to see its completion, and it is to his memory that I would like to dedicate this book.

Diana Schutz
Portland, Oregon

AUTOBIOBIOS

SERGIO ARAGONÉS
Well known for his humorous marginal strips in Mad magazine, multiple Eisner and Harvey Award-winning creator Sergio Aragonés has enjoyed forty years of success in the world of comics. His popular creator-owned comic, *Groo*, has now been in print for almost two decades, and the artist continues to lampoon every subject under the sun in such titles as *Boogeyman*, *Louder Than Words*, and *Actions Speak*.

EDDIE CAMPBELL
Eddie Campbell, multi-award winning artist of the groundbreaking *From Hell*, is the writer and artist of nine volumes of *Bacchus*, plus his *Alec* series, which includes *How to Be an Artist*, *After the Snooter*, *The King Canute Crowd*, and *Three Piece Suit*. Additional projects include Alan Moore's *Snakes & Ladders* and *The Birth Caul*, as well as *Hellblazer*, *Uncanny X-Men*, and Will Eisner's *The Spirit: The New Adventures*. He has also painted a *Batman* one-shot for DC Comics that he cowrote with Daren White.

PAUL CHADWICK
Paul Chadwick grew up in Washington State and earned a B.F.A. In illustration at Art Center College of Design in 1979. He worked in the movie business, storyboarding and doing advertising, before pencilling *Dazzler* for Marvel in 1984-'85. The next year he premiered *Concrete* in the first issue of Dark Horse Presents . Numerous *Concrete* stories have appeared there since, as well as in Concrete's own comics and books. Other works include *The World Below*, *Gifts of the Night*, and (with Harlan Ellison) *Seven Against Chaos*.

FAREL DALRYMPLE
Xeric Grant-winning cartoonist Farel Dalrymple self-published his staggeringly beautiful book *pop gun war*—a surreal tale of hope and redemption set against an urban landscape—until it was picked up by Absence of Ink Press and then collected in graphic novel form by Dark Horse. A Russ Manning Award nominee, Dalrymple won a 2002 Gold Medal from the Society of Illustrators.

RICHARD DOUTT
Richard Doutt has been a landscaper, carpenter, mechanic, and recluse, among other things. He has been married and has been homeless. These days, Doutt is a grandfather and an art student.

"The Tree" was written for a class on comics, taught by Diana Schutz. He is honored to be associated with Farel Dalrymple on this project and to be included here with some of the finest cartoonists in the world.

WILL EISNER
Will Eisner is universally acknowledged as one of the great masters of comic book art. Best known for his newspaper comics feature, *The Spirit*, which was syndicated worldwide for a dozen years, Eisner has enjoyed a long and winding career in narrative art. After a stint producing P.S. Magazine for the U.S. Army, Eisner returned to comics and since has produced numerous graphic novels, such as *A Contract With God* and, most recently, *Fagin the Jew*.

PAUL HORNSCHEMEIER
The Ignatz, Eisner, and Harvey Award-nominated creator of *Forlorn Funnies*, Paul Hornschemeier began working on comics while in college, self-publishing his experimental comics series, *Sequential* . His most recent book is the poignant collection of the *Forlorn Funnies* story arc, *Mother, Come Home*.

DAN JACKSON
Dan Jackson is the poster boy for multitasking. He digitally colors, inks, corrects, repairs, and occasionally letters comics on a daily and freelance basis for Dark Horse Comics. He also has the most amazing wife of anyone he knows and the cutest little girl in all the known world.

SEAN KONOT
Letterer Sean Konot has worked with a variety of publishers, including DC, Dark Horse, Maximum Press, Oni Press, and Image. Among his credits are such fan favorites as *Hellboy*, *Star Wars Tales*, *Green Arrow*, *Green Lantern*, *Harley Quinn*, and *Clerks*. Konot has also lettered stories featuring the characters Batman, Grendel, Catwoman, and Ghost.

JASON LUTES
After graduating from the Rhode Island School of Design in 1991, Jason Lutes moved to Seattle, where he drew a serialized comic called "Jar of Fools" for *The Stranger*, a weekly paper. The collected edition of this story is now in its fourth printing through Drawn & Quarterly, which also publishes installments of his on-

going comics novel *Berlin*, a portrait of the German city between the wars. "Rules to Live By" was created during the year he spent in Asheville, NC, before moving back to Seattle in the interest of a lifelong commitment to another person.

METAPHROG

Metaphrog, the Franco-Scottish duo, has been releasing comics since 1996, first serializing *Strange Weather Lately* and *The Maze*. Their current works, including *Louis: Red Letter Day*, *Louis: Lying to Clive*, and *Louis: The Clown's Last Words*, have received multiple Eisner and Ignatz Award nominations and critical acclaim worldwide.

FÁBIO MOON & GABRIEL BÁ

This duo started drawing comics in 1994, successfully failed at the superhero genre, and so moved on to do their own stories. They have now published two books in Brazil, have short stories in three other anthologies, and have been part of an art show in Spain about new Brazilian comics. Identical twins, Moon and Bá have won awards in Brazil for their independent publications, and received the Xeric Foundation Grant in 1999 to publish the miniseries *Roland: Days of Wrath*, written and self-published by Shane Amaya in the U.S.

BILL MORRISON

From car manual technical studies to advertising to painting some of Disney's most popular animated movie posters, Eisner Award–winning Bill Morrison has been a professional illustrator since 1981. He was recruited to draw *The Simpsons* in 1990, and has served as editor, a principal writer, and artist at Bongo Comics since 1994. Fulfilling a lifelong dream, Morrison contributed to Dark Horse's line of Tex Avery titles. As a Creative Director for Bongo, he was also an art ndirector for Fox's hit animated TV series, *Futurama*.

ARNOLD PANDER

Arnold Pander has been exploring the limits of multimedia, film, and comics with his brother, Jacob, since the Portland, Oregon underground music era of the '80s. They gained national attention in 1986 with Comico's *Grendel*, which led to such works as *Ginger Fox* and the internationally banned *Exquisite Corpse*. In 1990 they co-founded The Fuse Gallery, a collective of Portland art and performance spaces, and, in 1998, the production company Radius Pictures. Along with Arnold's 1997 Secret Broadcast, a CD inspired by pirate radio, the brothers have teamed up to depict futuristic cityscapes in Vertigo's *Accelerate* and the ambitious *Triple • X* for Dark Horse.

STAN SAKAI

Stan Sakai was born in Kyoto, Japan, grew up in Hawaii, and moved to California with his wife, Sharon, and two children, Hannah and Matthew. His creation, *Usagi Yojimbo*, first appeared in comics in 1984. Since then, Usagi has been on television as a guest of the Teenage Mutant Ninja Turtles and has been made into toys, seen on clothing, and featured in a series of trade paperback collections. Sakai is also an award-winning letterer for his work on the *Spider-Man* Sunday newspaper strips, *Usagi Yojimbo*, and Sergio Aragonés' *Groo the Wanderer*. Sakai is a recipient of a Parents' Choice Award, an Inkpot Award, multiple Eisner Awards, an American Library Association Award, a National Cartoonists Society Comic Book Division Award, and two Spanish Haxtur Awards.

DIANA SCHUTZ

Diana Schutz is a former editor-in-chief at Dark Horse Comics and adjunct instructor of comics history and criticism at Portland Community College.

WILLIAM STOUT

William Stout has worked as a designer on over thirty feature films. He has also been the key creator for a variety of Disney, Lucasfilm/Industrial Light and Magic, MCA/Universal, and DreamWorks SKG projects. Stout is perhaps best known for his depictions of dinosaurs that have been published and exhibited in museums worldwide, inspiring both *The Land Before Time* and *Jurassic Park*. His illustration work has won a host of honors, including two Gold Awards and one Silver Award from the Society of Illustrators. He has also written and illustrated the first visual history of life in Antarctica.

MATT WAGNER

Matt Wagner is best known for his highly respected creator-owned titles, *Grendel* and *Mage*, but he has also worked on *Sandman Mystery Theatre*, two successive *Batman/Grendel* crossovers as well as various other *Batman* titles, and a run of covers for the *Lone Wolf and Cub* series. In 1998 Wagner returned to the Hunter Rose incarnation of *Grendel*, in the multiple Eisner Award–winning miniseries–*Grendel: Black, White, & Red*–and followed with *Grendel: Red, White, & Black*, while also painting covers for DC's *Green Arrow* series. His later projects include DC's best-selling and critically acclaimed *Trinity*.

GABRIEL BÁ AND FÁBIO MOON!

"Twin Brazilian artists Fábio Moon and Gabriel Bá have made a huge mark on comics." —*Publisher's Weekly*

TWO BROTHERS
Story and art by Gabriel Bá
and Fábio Moon
ISBN 978-1-61655-856-7 | $24.99

DE:TALES
Story and art by Gabriel Bá
and Fábio Moon
ISBN 978-1-59582-557-5 | $19.99

THE UMBRELLA ACADEMY:
APOCALYPSE SUITE
Story by Gerard Way
Art by Gabriel Bá
TPB ISBN: 978-1-59307-978-9 | $17.99
Ltd. Ed. HC ISBN: 978-1-59582-163-8 | $79.95
Library Edition HC ISBN:
978-1-50671-547-6 | $39.99

THE UMBRELLA ACADEMY:
DALLAS
Story by Gerard Way
Art by Gabriel Bá
TPB ISBN: 978-1-59582-345-8 | $17.99
Ltd. Ed. HC ISBN: 978-1-59582-344-1 | $79.95
Library Edition HC ISBN:
978-1-50671-548-3 | $39.99

THE UMBRELLA ACADEMY:
HOTEL OBLIVION
Story by Gerard Way
Art by Gabriel Bá
TPB ISBN 978-1-50671-142-3 | $19.99

PIXU: THE MARK OF EVIL
Story and art by Gabriel Bá, Becky
Cloonan, Vasilis Lolos, and Fábio Moon
ISBN 978-1-61655-813-0 | $14.99

B.P.R.D.: VAMPIRE
Story by Mike Mignola,
Fábio Moon, and Gabriel Bá
Art by Fábio Moon and Gabriel Bá
ISBN 978-1-61655-196-4 | $19.99

B.P.R.D.: 1946–1948
Story by Mike Mignola,
Joshua Dysart, and John Arcudi
Art by Fábio Moon, Gabriel Bá,
Paul Azaceta, and Max Fiumara
ISBN 978-1-61655-646-4 | $34.99

NEIL GAIMAN'S HOW TO
TALK TO GIRLS AT PARTIES
Story by Neil Gaiman
Art by Fábio Moon and Gabriel Bá
978-1-61655-955-7 | $17.99